The Complete Academic SEARCH MANUAL

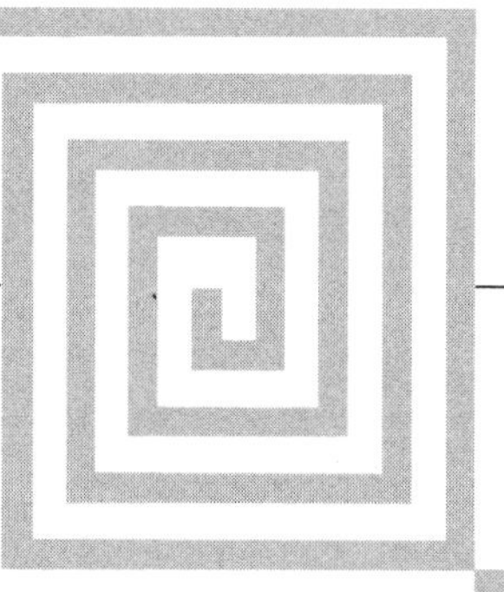

The Complete Academic SEARCH MANUAL

A Systematic Approach to Successful and Inclusive Hiring

LAUREN A. VICKER

and

HARRIETTE J. ROYER

STERLING, VIRGINIA

Published by Stylus Publishing, LLC
22883 Quicksilver Drive
Sterling, Virginia 20166-2102

Bulk Purchases
Quantity discounts are available for use in workshops and for staff development.
Call 1-800-232-0223

Book design and composition by Susan Mark
Coghill Composition Company
Richmond, Virginia

Library of Congress Cataloging-in-Publication-Data

Vicker, Lauren A., 1953–
The complete academic search manual : a systematic approach to successful and inclusive hiring / Lauren A. Vicker and Harriette J. Royer.—1st ed.
p. cm.
ISBN 1-57922-136-X (hardcover : alk. paper)—
ISBN 1-57922-139-4 (pbk. : alk. paper)
1. College teachers—Selection and appointment—United States—Handbooks, manuals, etc. 2. Universities and colleges—Faculty—Employment—United States—Handbooks, manuals, etc. 3. College administrators—Selection and appointment—United States—Handbooks, manuals, etc. I. Royer, Harriette J., 1945– II. Title.

LB2331.72.V53 2005
650.14'088'378—dc22

2005012114

ISBN: 1-57922-136-X (cloth)
ISBN: 1-57922-139-4 (paper)

Printed in the United States of America

All first editions printed on acid-free paper that meets the
American National Standards Institute Z39-48 Standard.

First Edition, 2006

10 9 8 7 6 5 4 3 2 1

To Jim and Greg for their
support and encouragement
at every step of the process.

Contents

Acknowledgments

WE ARE GRATEFUL to many people who helped us through the process of putting this work together.

From St. John Fisher College:

We thank Dr. Tim Franz of the Psychology Department for reviewing the earliest draft and providing excellent feedback and support for the work. We thank Dr. Ron Ambrosetti, Provost, and Dr. Jim Seward, Communication/Journalism, for supporting Lauren's sabbatical leave which made this effort possible. Many thanks to Dr. Arlette Miller-Smith, Dean of Diversity, Karen Gagie and Lisa DeCarlo of Human Resources, and to Dr. Sam Walton, Dean of the School of Education, for providing resources that we could use.

From the University of Rochester:

We appreciate Mark Zupan, Dean of the William E. Simon Graduate School of Business, and Angela Petrucco, the Director of Simon's Career Management Center, for providing an encouraging environment and resources for Harriette's contributions to the book; and Barbara Saat, Manager of Human Resources at the University of Rochester, for lending her resources.

We especially want to acknowledge Carl Goodman, Founding Principal of the ISAAC Network and catalyst extraordinaire, for his dynamic interactions and enduring impact on our work, and William E. Pickett, past President of St. John Fisher College, who created the academic search committee opportunity from which our relationship and this effort evolved.

We received valuable support, feedback, and resources from those outside of our home institutions:

Dr. Jonathan Alger of Rutgers University; Dr. Caroline S. Turner of Arizona State University; Dr. Karen DePauw and Dr. Larry Hincker of Virginia Tech; Dr. Keith Kaufman from Portland State University; Dr. Lee Becker of the University of Georgia; Dr. Fred Bonner of the University of Texas, San Antonio; Dr. Mark Serva from the University of Delaware; Dr. LeVon Wilson of Western Carolina University; Cynthia Hudgins of the University of Michigan; Amanda Shaffer of Case Western Reserve University; Christine Clark and Diane Krejsa of the University of Maryland; Phillip Dixon and Dr. Barbara Hines from Howard University; Gail Smith Boldt from ArnoldSmith Associates; and Renee Baker from Rochester Institute of Technology.

Introduction

Harriette's Story

It was debatable who was more surprised that the college president selected me to head the Search Committee for the Vice President of Student Affairs—me or the search committee. At the time, I was a relatively new mid-manager of the Career Services Office, hardly the typical choice to chair a search at this level. Adding further fuel to the fire, I had never been a member of an academic search committee. The faculty selected for the committee were especially dismayed because of my status as a member of the administration as well as my inexperience. Fortunately, I didn't know what I didn't know. Enthusiastically I plunged into the assignment by thoroughly researching best practices in executive searches.

In the late 1980s, few resources existed on conducting academic searches. Campus expertise was limited. I tapped Lauren, whose expertise in interviewing was well-known. Corporate recruiters whom I knew offered valuable insights and suggestions on structuring a search process.

Confident of my information and armed with a process fused from several sources, I called the first meeting of the search committee. My assumption that the committee would embrace my leadership was immediately challenged. Neither the process I proposed nor my concept of the role of the committee, gleaned from my research, was accepted by the committee! Members disagreed about their roles, the goal of the search, and especially the need for a process. Several of the members declared that they needed only to read the resumés to select the final candidates. The president's charge to bring in diverse finalists was dismissed as a fantasy. Furthermore, the majority saw no reason for many meetings or a lot of discussion.

The committee members did consent to discussing the process, and after two contentious meetings, we agreed upon a process. The concept of using tools such as a timeline, position profiles, meeting protocols, stakeholder interviews, tracking spreadsheets, and interview protocols was adopted. These tools were developed and used for various steps in the process.

In spite of a rather rocky beginning, the tension and dissension expressed by the committee was resolved. The VP search concluded ahead of schedule, a first at the college, and under budget. The president was presented three finalists, two males and one female, two of whom were minority candidates. The caliber of the candidates impressed the committee, faculty, and staff who contributed to the interview process, and the president. The selected candidate catalyzed a significant shift in the role of Student Affairs at the college. Members of the search committee continued their cross-functional collaborations, contributing in many ways to the expansion of collegiality and the deepening of trust on campus. The involvement of a broad representation of the campus in the process caused dialogue and debate among faculty, staff, and students. Subsequently, other search committees requested assistance with their process. "Harriette's Process" was made available through the Human Resources Office, and Lauren consulted with them on interviewing. In one year, the search and selection process on the campus changed dramatically from that first meeting.

Among the many duties that fall on the shoulders of academic professionals, participating in an academic search to fill a faculty or administrative vacancy can be one of the most daunting. Many academics are thrust into the role with little preparation beyond their own experience of being interviewed for academic positions. However, a successful search process is integral to the mission of any department or college wishing to recruit and retain high caliber college faculty and administrators. This is especially true in lean economic times, when the supply of applicants may be plentiful. Inexperienced search committees may feel overwhelmed by the prospect of a complex and serious task and the consequences of an unsuccessful search. In addition, searches can be stressful in the context of the academic year, when faculty members are also teaching, advising, doing college service, and working on their own research.

Harriette's experience may strike a chord for faculty and administrators who

- Have just been appointed to their first search committee and feel unprepared
- Are reluctant to serve on a search committee because searches seem too structured and process driven
- Have been chosen to head a search and feel overwhelmed
- Have had such unpleasant experiences on search committees in the past that they avoid them at all costs

This guide will provide faculty members, department heads, chairs, and deans with a ten-step process for conducting searches for faculty and administrative positions. Using a proven, systematic process makes it easier for the committee members to work together and reach consensus on the final candidate. In addition, adding structure to the process will help you avoid pitfalls of possible EEO/AA (Equal Employment Opportunity/Affirmative Action) law violation.

The search process described here will be a valuable asset and a practical guide for any search committee. The process will expedite the search while optimizing the outcomes.

We recommend that you follow the ten steps in order, but the chapters are also designed to be used as stand-alone reference guides for individual topics. The ten steps are described in the following chapters:

- Chapter 1: Preparing the Search Committee
- Chapter 2: Profile and Position Descriptions
- Chapter 3: Recruiting Candidates
- Chapter 4: Evaluating Resumés
- Chapter 5: Preparing to Interview
- Chapter 6: Preliminary Screening Interviews
- Chapter 7: The Campus Interviews
- Chapter 8. Evaluating the Finalists
- Chapter 9: Negotiating and Making the Offer
- Chapter 10: Extending Hospitality to the New Hire

Throughout the process, we also address the issue of attracting a diverse candidate pool in your academic search. Despite the efforts of many colleges and universities, racial and ethnic minorities remain grossly underrepresented among college faculty, making up less than 14 percent nationwide (Turner, 2002). At the same time, the percentage of students of color attending college is growing rapidly. According to the U.S. Department of Education, the "baby boom echo" will increase the college population by 1.6 million students by 2015. Of that increase, 80 percent will be nonwhite and 50 percent will be Hispanic (Roach, 2001). Diversifying the faculty and administration will better serve this diverse population; make the climate on campus more friendly for students of color, thus increasing retention; and contribute directly to educational quality and improved educational outcomes for *all* students.

However, many colleges and universities find it challenging to solicit applications from traditionally underrepresented groups. Search committees need to increase their use of active over passive approaches to recruiting for more diversity among their faculty and administrators. According to faculty diversity expert Daryl Smith, the most important factors in successfully recruiting candidates of color include personal networking, strong leadership operating in a spirit of consensus with the search committee, championing of minority candidates by someone at the hiring institution, sensitivity to dual career couples, and post-hiring support (Smith, 1996). We address these factors throughout the book and offer some "Examples Worth Noting" that have worked successfully on a variety of college campuses.

Perhaps you have heard colleagues complain that serving on an academic or administrative search committee is a time-consuming, frustrating, and thankless job. We have found searches to be exciting, challenging, and satisfying. Many factors determine whether you have a positive or a negative experience. However, the use of a systematic search process, such as the one described here, will maximize your chances for success and satisfaction.

You are free to use and adapt the materials in this guide. If you don't see something you need for your specific search, we invite you to contact us. We also look forward to hearing from you about the success of your search process and the usefulness of the materials presented here. We'll respond to you promptly and provide you with our best advice and resources.

Contact us at academicsearch@yahoo.com

References

Roach, R. (2001). Is higher education ready for minority America? *Black Issues in Higher Education, 18*(8), 29–31.

Smith, D. G. (1996). *Achieving faculty diversity: Debunking the myths.* Washington, DC: Association of American Colleges and Universities.

Turner, C. S. (2002). *Diversifying the faculty: A guidebook for search committees.* Washington, DC: Association of American Colleges and Universities.

CHAPTER 1

Preparing the Search Committee

In this chapter, you will

- Learn the steps involved in selecting a representative and diverse search committee
- Review the role and function of the search committee
- Understand the duties of the chair and search committee members
- Refresh your understanding of consensus practices and agree to operate by consensus
- Determine procedures that will lay the foundation for your search

Getting Started

YOU'VE JUST BEEN APPOINTED to the search committee and enthusiasm is high. It's time for your first meeting, and everyone comes with individual perceptions, individual experiences, and individual expectations. This first meeting is critical because it lays the groundwork for the committee to function effectively for the rest of the search. A successful first meeting sets the stage for a successful search outcome. Resist the urge to plunge right in with suggestions on procedures, recruiting, interviewing, and the best places to take candidates for dinner. Instead, take the time to ensure that everyone is on the same page with regard to group membership, group processes, and group logistics. While the role of the chair is crucial, each member bears responsibility for getting the committee off to a positive start.

The Role and Composition of the Committee

A search committee is an integral component of an effective search for most faculty and administrative positions. The search process typically begins with appointing the search committee. While procedures vary among institutions and even among departments within institutions, the role of the search committee is to oversee the entire recruitment process and participate proactively in the selection process. The committee is typically charged with developing a position description, writing and distributing the advertisements, screening applicants, interviewing candidates, and presenting the finalists to the hiring authority—the person who commissions the search.

To be effective, the search committee must be large enough to represent a diversity of opinion and constituencies, but not so big that members do not feel part of the group. Expert opinions vary, but we have found that a search committee of five to nine members can function effectively in most situations. With fewer than five people, the committee may not get a wide enough scope of input and perspectives. With more than nine people, logistics may be difficult and coalitions may form too easily. For some small departments, the search committee may actually be a "committee of the whole," where everyone serves. The key here is to be sure that your search committee is diverse enough to represent the diversity needs of the institution, staff, and students, and to attract candidates that represent a diverse pool.

For example, in a search for a marketing professor, the committee may include two professors who teach in the marketing area, a professor from another area of the business department, an administrator with marketing responsibilities—the Director of Admissions or Public Relations—and an outside faculty member with an interest in the position—perhaps an Advertising professor—or even an alumnus who is distinguished in the field. In some schools where students are also invited to serve on search committees, the president of the marketing club could be tapped.

If none of the above committee members are people of color or female, an individual from another academic or co-curricular area might be selected. Turner reports that some institutions have invited doctoral graduates of color and scholars of color from neighboring institutions or disciplinary associations to join search committees. She notes that reaching out to these colleagues may not only diversify the current search committee, but may also yield longer term benefits to graduate student recruitment, intern and graduate placement, and research collaboration (Turner, 2002, p. 14). See the box below for an example of instructions about diversity composition to a search committee.

The composition of the search committee may also be influenced by guidelines provided by your institution. Some schools, such as Portland State University, have actually established hiring resource teams that provide guidelines for recruiting, hiring, and retaining diverse faculty and staff. A number of larger institutions have a Diversity or Equal Opportunity Office that actively consults with faculty and administration search committees. At many institutions, representation of women and minorities is required on search committees. Be sure to check with your Human Resources or Diversity Office to see if any specific guidelines apply to your search committee.

The Committee Chair and the Members

In some academic searches, the chair is appointed by the person commissioning the search. For example, the president may appoint the chair in the search for a new provost. In other searches, the chair is selected from among the members of the committee. Either way, the roles and responsibilities of the chair, vice-chair, and other members need to be laid out and agreed upon at the outset. Regardless of how the chair is selected, it is important that the person assuming the role understands and accepts his or her responsibilities. The list on page 3 captures the fundamental responsibilities that the search committee chair must manage or delegate.

An Example Worth Noting: Committee Composition

The University of Maryland, a noted leader in diversity hiring in academia, gives the following instructions to search committees regarding representation of diverse constituencies:

> Because search committees play pivotal roles in diversifying campus faculty and staff, it is important that they include representation from underrepresented groups. Such persons can provide diverse perspectives and access to non-traditional networks and contacts, as well as lending general expertise and credibility to the work of the committee. It is important that committee members from underrepresented groups be of the same general rank or status as other members of the committee and have general familiarity with the position and with the unit doing the hiring. Ideally, such representation can come from within the staff in the unit; if no one is available, *every effort should be made to identify persons from other units* who have the expertise and time to serve on the committee. While student representation on committees may be required or desired, *students should not be expected to serve as the lone representatives of diversity on campus search committees.* Such a practice inherently places the students at a distinct disadvantage, whether undergraduate or graduate, and serves neither the interests of the hiring unit nor the campus affirmative action goals.

Responsibilities of the Search Committee Chair

- Create a climate of trust, mutual respect, and consensus building.
- Call the meetings.
- Organize the agendas.
- Ensure that process notes are shared promptly.
- Facilitate all meetings so that the agenda items are addressed within the time frame.
- Move the process forward according to the time line.
- Communicate with the person who charged the committee regarding progress.
- Ensure that all documentation expected in the search is completed accurately, on time, and delivered to the designated personnel on time.
- Delegate key responsibilities such as administrative support, schedules, and candidate visits as appropriate.
- Act as spokesperson for the committee to internal and external constituencies.
- Address/confront conflicts of interest and other issues that surface during the search process.
- Present the final candidate(s) to the person who charged the committee.
- Encourage a process for welcoming the new hire.

When the convener of the search committee invites each member to join, it is important to review the responsibilities of the general members, too. While it is an honor to be selected for the committee, it is also a considerable responsibility and time commitment. The commitments of committee members should be clearly understood by all. See this page for the ones we have used.

Understanding the Charge to the Committee

At the first meeting, the search committee needs to address the charge, the role of the committee, and the relationship of the position to the institution. In many universities, the person who charged the committee presents the formal charge to the search committee in

Responsibilities of Search Committee Members

- Attend all the meetings.
- Complete assignments on time.
- Contribute your personal and professional perspectives.
- Sustain the vision for the position, keeping the best interest of the department and the institution in mind.
- Communicate your opinions honestly to other members.
- Speak candidly with candidates while maintaining a positive attitude about the position, department, and institution.
- Work toward consensus.
- Respect the confidentiality of the process as well as that of each candidate and the department.
- Abide by the agreements made by the full committee, even if you do not fully support them.

writing or in person at the first meeting. The search committee may be charged with presenting a slate of candidates in rank order, a slate of candidates in no order, or a single candidate for the position. Within academic departments, some committees make the final decision, while others recommend to the administration, which will make the final offer.

At Case Western Reserve University, for example, the search committee charge covers the following essential factors:

- The position to be filled with an attached job description
- The tasks and role of the committee in the search
- The scope of the search (e.g., internal, local, national, international)
- Deadline for presenting recommendations from the committee
- Affirmative action considerations
- Statement of confidentiality practices at each stage of the search

Agreeing on Shared Values

It can't be assumed that we all share the same values. Therefore, the committee must discuss the values that will guide its search. A department mission statement, a college strategic plan, and an honest and open discussion are all ways to identify shared values. At a minimum, we have found these shared values to be indispensable:

- Respect for each other and for the candidates in the process
- Commitment to teamwork
- Open-mindedness—willingness to share and consider divergent opinions
- Strict confidentiality to protect the committee members as well as the candidates throughout the process
- Commitment to consensus
- Agreement to honor commitments (e.g., attending meetings, respecting deadlines)

Additionally, the committee needs to confront the issue of diversity in its position announcement and recruitment of candidates. This is discussed further in subsequent chapters.

Agreeing on the Process

The entire search committee must agree to work as a team with the goal of achieving consensus at the conclusion of the process. Planning ahead to vote by majority rule sets up a dangerous situation where coalitions may form and not everyone will feel committed to the process or the final selection. To aid in consensus building, the committee should decide on a systematic process early on. Your college may have a process in place that enumerates the steps a search committee will go through. If it does, the committee should review that process to be sure it fits the needs of the current search. If it does not, the committee needs to agree upon steps it will take to ensure a successful search. The steps outlined in this manual present a proven process for the committee to adapt and use. Agreeing on the process in this early stage will save time and avoid conflict as the search progresses—the structure is in place and the committee agrees to work through that structure to its conclusion.

There are many ways that groups make decisions: by the leader, by majority rule, by compromise, and by consensus. In a search process, consensus is the optimal decision-making technique, since all group members accept and support the decision. Successful search committees cultivate consensus building throughout each step of the process. Working as a team and reaching agreement at each step will make it more likely that the search committee will identify and support a consensus candidate at the end. As you begin to set the initial procedures that will guide you throughout the search, it is wise to familiarize yourselves with proven practices for reaching consensus and adopt a shared process. By working to achieve consensus now, you will develop a habit of consensus building that you can apply throughout the search.

The chair might consider reviewing with the group the Consensus Guidelines from Engleberg and Wynn (2003). The elements of this model are outlined on page 5.

By following a group discussion model that considers consensus the most desirable way to make decisions, the search committee establishes a solid foundation for the myriad decisions it has to make throughout the process. While it is not always possible to achieve consensus on every decision, the intent and effort to gain support and agreement among group members builds group cohesion and cooperation.

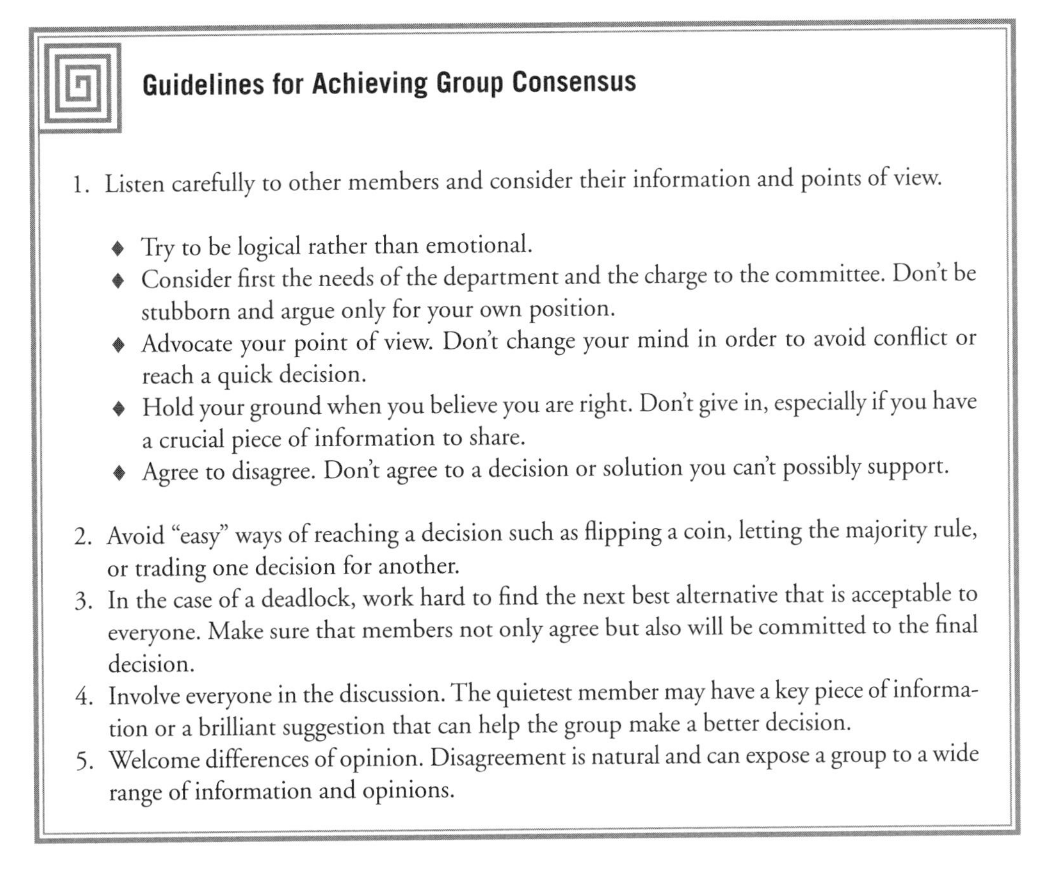

Guidelines for Achieving Group Consensus

1. Listen carefully to other members and consider their information and points of view.

    - ♦ Try to be logical rather than emotional.
    - ♦ Consider first the needs of the department and the charge to the committee. Don't be stubborn and argue only for your own position.
    - ♦ Advocate your point of view. Don't change your mind in order to avoid conflict or reach a quick decision.
    - ♦ Hold your ground when you believe you are right. Don't give in, especially if you have a crucial piece of information to share.
    - ♦ Agree to disagree. Don't agree to a decision or solution you can't possibly support.

2. Avoid "easy" ways of reaching a decision such as flipping a coin, letting the majority rule, or trading one decision for another.
3. In the case of a deadlock, work hard to find the next best alternative that is acceptable to everyone. Make sure that members not only agree but also will be committed to the final decision.
4. Involve everyone in the discussion. The quietest member may have a key piece of information or a brilliant suggestion that can help the group make a better decision.
5. Welcome differences of opinion. Disagreement is natural and can expose a group to a wide range of information and opinions.

Agreeing on Logistics

Search committee members must be flexible and willing to adjust their schedules to make the process work. Resumé reviews, phone interviews, interview planning, candidate campus visits, and candidate reviews all take time. The group must also have a clear understanding of the use of administrative support, budget, availability of meeting rooms, and use of software and equipment. Creating a timeline for the completion of the process is also desirable at this early stage. A sample timeline used in an academic search appears on page 6.

Setting up Tracking and Communication Systems

A serious oversight made by many search committees is the failure to track applicants from the very start of the process. The purposes of tracking are to keep the committee and the institution updated and informed about the status of every candidate in the process, and to communicate with applicants in a timely manner. We recommend that you immediately establish a competent and easy-to-implement tracking system for a number of reasons. Tracking all applicants, and in particular those who represent a diverse candidate pool, helps to maintain the integrity of the process and the high standards of the institution, minimizing the risk that an applicant falls through the cracks. A great deal of ill will is created if an application is not acknowledged or the applicants are not informed of their status in the process. A lack of communication can come back to haunt an institution. Another compelling reason to establish a tracking system is to comply with government oversight. Institutions that receive federal funding are typically required to track the gender, race, and status of all applicants and submit the documentation for government scrutiny upon request.

The committee must decide what to track as the search progresses, as well as how to track the key information about the candidates. Such tracking information may include date of application, date of responses and all communications, contacts with references, phone interviews, campus interviews, gender, ethnicity, and disposition of the application with the reason.

Sample Timeline: Journalism Professor

Step	*Month*	*Description*
1	April	Organizing the committee and research
2	May	Position description
3	June–Aug	Recruiting candidates • *AEJMC* News*: June 1 deadline for convention in August • Websites for minority groups in the field: August • *Chronicle*: August • Networking: personal contacts, targeting chairs of graduate programs
4	By Oct 15	Evaluating resumés
5	Nov 15	Preliminary screening • *AEJMC** in August • Phone screens by Nov 15
6	mid-Nov	Preparing for the campus interviews
7	Nov–Dec	Conducting the campus interviews
8	mid-Dec	Evaluating finalists
9	Feb	Making and confirming the offer, announcing the hire
10	Aug	Welcoming the new hire

*Association for Educators in Journalism and Mass Communication—newsletter and convention.

Tracking can be done using a Microsoft Excel spreadsheet, an Access database, or simply a Word table. A sample tracking form is provided here to use as a guide.

The committee must also decide how it will share materials. With multiple members and numerous applicants, it is important that this responsibility is both a shared experience and an orderly process. Many in-

Sample Tracking Form

Name	Contact Info	Date of Application/ Source	Gender, Race	Acknowledge Application	Phone Screen	Campus Interview	Outcome/ Reason	Notified

stitutions favor Microsoft Outlook, while classroom management programs like Blackboard or Angel are successfully employed by others with access restricted to search committee members.

Potential Pitfall: Deciding Whether You Need Outside Help

Some search committees with high-level charges may choose to employ a search consultant. Consultants who specialize in academic searches can be very successful at setting up and conducting the entire process. They are also likely to identify attractive candidates who might not have been actively applying for positions. In a recent provost search at a liberal arts college, three of the four finalists were not actively searching but were recruited by the consultant. On the other hand, the cost of using consultants may be prohibitive, especially for a faculty search within a single academic department.

We have found a rich and ready reserve of expertise in academic, administrative, and technology departments on our campuses, including Human Resources and the Career Services Office. Take advantage of them!

CHECKLIST FOR PREPARING THE SEARCH COMMITTEE

- ❒ Selected committee members:
  - constituency represented: ____________________
  - constituency represented: ____________________
  - constituency represented: ____________________
  - constituency represented: ____________________
- ❒ Assured representation of diversity perspectives
- ❒ Selected chair
- ❒ Reviewed responsibilities of chair and members
- ❒ Reviewed guidelines for operating by consensus
- ❒ Discussed and agreed upon charge to the committee
- ❒ Discussed and agreed upon values
- ❒ Discussed and agreed upon process
- ❒ Agreed on time line
- ❒ Determined tracking system

References

Engleberg, I. N., & Wynn, D. R. (2003). *Working in groups: Principles and strategies* (3rd ed.). Boston: Houghton-Mifflin, p. 206.

Faculty Search Guidelines (2004–2005). *The search committee, the committee charge*, retrieved 02-25-05 from http://www.cwru.edu/president/aaction/guide.html#charge

Turner, C. S. (2002). *Diversifying the faculty: A guidebook for search committees.* Washington, DC: Association of American Colleges and Universities.

University of Maryland Diversity Database. *Moving toward community, procedures and guidelines for conducting faculty and staff searches at UMCP*, Chapter 2, The Search Committee (September, 1999). Retrieved 02/24/05 from http://www.inform.umd.edu/EdRes/Topic/Diversity/Response/UM/Proc/chap2.html

CHAPTER 2

Profile and Position Descriptions

In this chapter, you will

- Learn the procedure for interviewing stakeholders
- Create a profile which will guide your work throughout the process
- Formulate a compelling and cogent position description that will encourage applications from a diverse applicant pool
- Compose a compelling ad, announcing the open position
- Consider critical pitfalls that may undermine your work in its early stages

Getting Started

IN OUR EXPERIENCE, formulating the profile and position description is a pivotal step in the process, yet it is often the most neglected and unappreciated by search committees and those charging them. A search process is like a treasure hunt. The success of the hunters in quickly locating the treasure is a direct measure of the detail and accuracy of their map. Once they arrive at their destination, their ability to identify the treasure relies upon the vividness of their picture of the treasure. By thoroughly researching and defining the scope, vision, accountabilities, and candidate qualifications of a vacant position, a search committee can wield considerable influence over the direction and future effectiveness of a department or institution.

This stage of the committee's work is intense. It requires a process for gathering and recording a mountain of complex, sometimes conflicting, information. A few meetings may be necessary to come to consensus about the purpose, accountabilities, and requirements of the position and the preferred candidate qualifications. The process may even uncover structural or leadership issues in the department that should be resolved before the search can be launched. However, the committee that best executes its charge establishes a systematic process and scrupulously executes it. To do less is to cheat the institution of excellent administrative and academic talent.

Researching Responsibilities and Needs

Start with researching the current responsibilities and emerging needs impacting this position. One or two members of the search committee can easily handle this assignment. Develop a simple interview form to keep your conversations focused on the important topics.

Begin by reading the operative job description. This provides you with a baseline indicating how the job was envisioned and executed in the past. Ask yourself, "What does this position accomplish? To what end? For whom?" Record your perceptions.

It's important to consult the key stakeholders. This step can be accomplished in person, by phone, or via e-mail. Interview the person who charged the search committee about her or his expectations of the position and qualities desired in the candidate selected. Ask questions about how the position fits in the bigger picture of the department, division, and institution. See page 10 for a list of questions.

Occasionally search committees decide to interview one or two incumbents from benchmark institutions to gain further insights and a broader perspective about the position.

Questions to Ask Stakeholders

- How does this position support the department and its mission?
- What expectations do you have for the person in this position?
- What do you think the committee should be looking for in a candidate?
- What opportunities related to this position have been overlooked in the past as possible growth areas?
- What characteristics are you looking for in a candidate who would be an excellent fit?
- What emerging trends and challenges in the field do you see that will impact this position?

In your institution, are students considered key stakeholders? Consider inviting a group of students to an information-gathering forum. Ask their opinions about the position and function. Probe them about ways in which the role could contribute more robustly to satisfying their expectations. In our experience, the views of the constituents provide the committee with valuable perspectives that may lead to break-through perceptions about the position.

It is crucial at this early step to consider the possibility that the needs of this position and the desirable qualifications for the job may have changed. Don't fall into the trap of assuming you are hiring for "more of the same." Dynamic departments and institutions are looking for ways to improve and grow with each new hire.

Creating the Position Description

Creating the position description begins by synthesizing the research you have gathered and organizing the details of the position. The position description elaborates the "what" of the position: its key functions, essential responsibilities, critical accountabilities, and its role within the organization. Applicants use it to judge whether to pursue the position and the committee uses it to compare and evaluate candidates.

The basic elements of a position description include the following:

- A statement of the purpose of the position
- Elaboration on the essential functions and primary interfaces
- Delineation of the required and preferred qualifications
- A statement about terms and compensation (EEO/AA).

An example of a position description for an Assistant Director of Career Services appears on page 11. Additional examples of administrative and academic position descriptions at various levels can be readily obtained on *The Chronicle of Higher Education* website.

Creating the Profile

Where the position description elaborates on the function and expectations of the position, the profile elaborates on the qualities of the ideal candidate to fill the position. It serves a function different from the position description—it answers the question, "What knowledge, traits, experience, and personal qualities will it take to succeed in this position as we have defined it?" By contrast, you may find it useful to ask, "What are the traits, experiences, and abilities we *don't* want?" The development of the profile is your opportunity to break down the typical prejudices that lock out otherwise qualified candidates, particularly diversity candidates. Our tendency is to find the person who most resembles (or in some cases is the most divergent from) the former incumbent, and in doing so we eliminate applicants who could very well lead the charge for change. The key here is to create a profile that captures in detail the features of the perfect candidate. Applicants will never see the profile. The search committee uses it to assess the information offered by applicants in

Assistant Director of Career Services Job Description

The Assistant Director of Career Development is responsible for the development and implementation of the student-focused and campus-based four-year development program related to the job search process, career opportunities and recruitment to prepare students for life in the twenty-first century. Responsibilities include but are not limited to career counseling, library resource development, interview and resumé preparation, and coordination of all aspects of the internship program. The assistant director will work with students, staff, faculty, alumni, and employers to create and present career workshops, programs in residence halls, career and job fairs, panel discussions, newsletters, video productions, statistical tracking, and peer advising programs, as well as to manage the student database and the web-based career board.

Qualifications: BA required, MA preferred with coursework in counseling, student personnel, or related field. Preference for career counseling skills; vocational testing expertise; computer proficiency (web and database); effective oral and written skills; ability to establish rapport with multicultural students, faculty, alumni, employers, and staff in a liberal arts environment; academic experiences with and interests in culturally diverse groups. EOE/AA—Women and underrepresented groups are encouraged to apply.

their resumés and cover letters and to make qualitative judgments about their qualifications for the position.

The profile for the Assistant Director of Career Services on page 12 illustrates the differences between the position description and the profile.

Developing a profile is not a typical step in higher education. Quite commonly search committee members tell us, "We'll know the best candidates when we see their resumés." From our experience, that doesn't happen. That mind-set is like looking for the keys you lost, not in the dark driveway where you dropped them, but across the street because the lighting is better. The best candidate may be where the keys landed, not where the search committee is looking.

The exercise of creating the position description and the profile occasionally uncovers organizational or perceptual discrepancies. These become the fertile fields for dialogue. The committee, in consultation with the person who charged the committee, needs to resolve the discrepancies and create the vision for the position and the candidate. By focusing on these areas, the committee will evolve sharper distinctions about the position, clarify the preferred qualifications of the candidate, and illuminate the opportunities for driving change in the organization.

Capturing the Allure

Capturing the allure drives your advertising communications and guides conversations promoting the opportunity with the applicants. A thorough profile and position description naturally leads the search committee to envisage who would want to do the job, at what stage of their career they would be, and where they are likely to be found. You will answer questions such as:

- What are we offering that would attract top candidates?
- What compensation package would attract this kind of candidate?
- What are the critical selling points of our opportunity, institution, and community?

Compile the responses to these questions and make a list of all the distinct factors you can identify.

Wise search committees involve key stakeholders in reacting to the final draft of both the position description and profile, and get their "take" on the critical selling points. In doing so, you are likely to secure their buy-in, stir up anticipation about the position, and stimulate referrals. By taking this extra step, you are also

Profile: Assistant Director of Career Services

Critical Dimensions	*Evidence*
Counseling:	Is approachable, warm, and comfortable with you and others. Projects a student-centered approach to counseling. Listens well. Expresses belief that the student is in control of his/her life. Sees the counselor role as helping students understand themselves, providing structure, support and resources; challenging beliefs and nonproductive behaviors; teaching skills; coaching new behaviors; interpreting workplace expectations.
Programming:	Demonstrates the ability to handle many tasks at once. Attends to details without losing "the big picture." Coordinates programs by accurately checking processes and tasks over time; delegates appropriately. Evaluates programs and makes improvements based on results. Is "customer focused"—tuned into career needs of college students and what they will respond to. Cites evidence of experience working with diverse groups of students, including women and disabled students. Successfully markets programs as measured by responses of intended participants. Is a self-starting, proactive planner. Demonstrates evidence of creativity in promoting and marketing to students and employers.
Recruiting:	Projects a professional demeanor and image—you could see this person representing the college to employers. Is "customer focused"—demonstrates knowledge of the expectations of prospective employers of college graduates, gives evidence of a track record developing employer relations that produce results. Presents a compelling and flawless resumé. Interviews well.
Teamwork:	Experienced in working on a team. Expresses concern for the "common good." Gives evidence of leadership and followership, cooperation and collaboration, concern for the positive outcome of an activity and willingness to do what needs to be done to accomplish a goal. Is considerate of the feelings and needs of others. Provides evidence of collaboration with faculty, students, other administrative areas, employers, and colleagues from other institutions.

more likely to improve the chances of attracting a more diverse applicant pool.

Creating a Compelling Advertisement

Composing a compelling advertisement heightens the odds that you will attract the applicant pool you desire. Begin by synthesizing the salient elements from both the profile and the position description that distinguish your opportunity. Look up comparable position descriptions in the *The Chronicle.* Notice what sets them apart and what makes them appealing or unappealing. Highlight the distinguishing features that will make your ad compelling.

The cost of advertising may influence the length of your announcement. Using the elements listed on page 13, create both a detailed and a short advertisement. The Human Resources office may be able to assist you in this step. The detailed announcement can be displayed on the institution's website and the short one used for print and online advertisement. Examples follow at the end of this chapter.

Wording Your Ad to Attract Diverse Applicants

How your ad is worded may also impact the diversity of applicants you attract. One of the critical errors that a search committee can make at this stage is wording the ad in too structured a way. Institutions that have been successful at recruiting diverse applicant pools for their faculty and administrative openings have demonstrated flexibility in their position announcements. For example, the University of Maryland provides its search committees ways to use flexible wording to improve outreach to minority applicants:

- "Candidates should posses an advanced degree, preferably the doctorate," rather than "Ph.D. required."

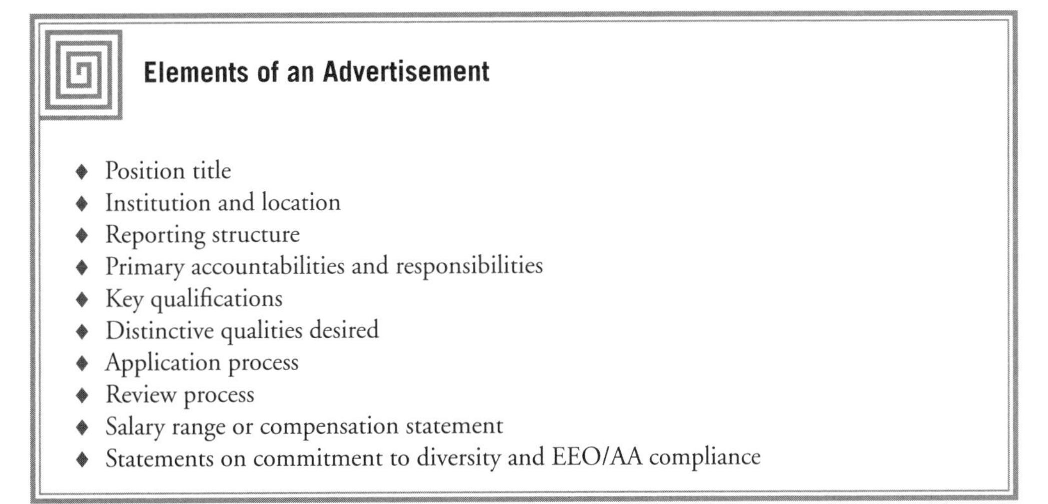

Elements of an Advertisement

- Position title
- Institution and location
- Reporting structure
- Primary accountabilities and responsibilities
- Key qualifications
- Distinctive qualities desired
- Application process
- Review process
- Salary range or compensation statement
- Statements on commitment to diversity and EEO/AA compliance

- "Candidates should have an advanced degree in counseling or a related discipline," rather than "degree in counseling required."
- "Candidates should have an MA degree and three years work experience, or BA degree and five years experience," rather than "an MA and three years work experience required."
- "Candidates should have a solid record of scholarship and research," rather than "candidates should have a distinguished or nationally recognized body of research and scholarships."

An emphasis on the interest in affirmative action candidates can be represented by strategic placement of the EEO/Affirmative Action statement. Placement within the body of the announcement, particularly as part of the listing of qualifications, indicates a high level of interest.

The University of Michigan suggests using these phrases:

- "The college is especially interested in qualified candidates who can contribute, through their research, teaching, and/or service, to the diversity and excellence of the academic community."
- "The University is responsive to the needs of dual career couples."
- "Women, minorities, individuals with disabilities, and veterans are encouraged to apply."

At Case Western Reserve University, all advertisements must include the statement: "In employment, as in education, Case Western Reserve University is committed to Equal Opportunity and World Class Diversity." In addition, search committees are instructed that the statement alone does not by itself make the university inviting or welcoming to women and minorities. The following phrases are suggested starting points for search committees to alert diversity applicants that their expertise is valued:

- "Interest in developing and implementing curricula that address multicultural issues."
- "Academic experiences and interests in culturally diverse groups."
- "Previous experience interacting with communities of color."
- "Experience with a variety of teaching methods and/or curricular perspectives."

At this stage, the search committee must make a conscious effort to appeal to a broad range of individuals in order to attract a diverse applicant pool. Let's look in more detail at Portland State University, a school that initially was unsuccessful in attracting diversity applicants for a faculty opening. We examine how the Psychology Department changed their ad to broaden its appeal and diversify the applicant pool in the Example Worth Noting on page 14.

The PSU example models the difference made by being intentionally more deliberate and explicit in position descriptions. According to Dr. Keith Kaufman, Psychology Department chair, the strategy successfully attracted

An Example Worth Noting: Converting a Typical Ad into an Ad that Attracts Diverse Applicants

Diversity goals at Portland State University are aggressively pursued by its Diversity Action Council (DAC) and its sub-groups, like the Hiring Resource Team and the Diversity Liaison Network. The Hiring Resource Team's function is to develop and promulgate effective strategies for recruiting, hiring, and retaining diverse faculty. Among the strategies they model for the university is the practice of tailoring the wording of job advertisements in such a way as to attract applicants from underrepresented groups. Their experience confirms that the applicant pool for positions can be expanded by broadening the areas the search committee is willing to consider, stating that experience working with students of diverse backgrounds is preferred, tailoring research and teaching needs to enhance curricular diversity, and strongly asserting the university's commitment to diversity in the ad.

A faculty opening in the Psychology Department yielded few minority applicants before Professor Keith Kaufman rewrote the position ad. Two examples follow, a "before" and an "after " with footnoted comments underlined by Dr. Kaufman.

Initial Ad

Assistant or Associate Professor in Applied Cognitive Psychology

The Department of Psychology at Portland State University has a tenure-track opening for an Assistant or Associate Professor in Applied Cognitive Psychology (1) beginning September 2000 or January 2001. A member of the Oregon University System, PSU is an urban grant university with a commitment to research and service in urban settings. The Department of Psychology has a strong applied research orientation with a commitment to looking at psychological problems in their systematic context. Our doctoral program in Systems Science Psychology includes areas of specialization in Applied Developmental, Industrial Organizational, and Applied Social Psychology.

Responsibilities for the position include productive scholarship in applied settings, teaching in areas of cognitive psychology (2) at undergraduate and graduate levels, grant writing, supervising dissertations and student practica, and participation in faculty governance. Qualifications include a doctoral degree and a commitment to theoretically based research. We are especially interested in applicants whose research overlaps with either applied development, applied social, industrial/organizational or quantitative psychology (3). In keeping with our university's mission regarding campus diversity, we particularly encourage members of historically underrepresented groups to apply (4).

Send letter of application, vita, at least three letters of reference, statement of applied interests and experience, copies of papers, and statement of teaching philosophy and interests to Cognitive Psychology Search Committee, Department of Psychology. Portland State University is an Affirmative Action/Equal Opportunity Institution (5).

Comments:

1. very narrow focus
2. very narrow scope of responsibility
3. narrow focus of research—requires overlap
4. weak, general diversity statement
5. canned phrase, appears insincere

Reworded Ad

Assistant or Associate Professor (1) Applied Psychologist

The Department of Psychology at Portland State University has a tenure-track opening beginning September 2000 or January 2001. The specific area of expertise within applied psychology is open but we are especially interested in individuals whose work matches the current focus in the department on developmental, industrial/organizational, social in field settings, cognitive, and community psychology (2). As an urban university, PSU is committed to scholarship and community outreach relevant to the needs of urban, metropolitan areas. Individuals with research and teaching interests relating to multiculturalism, ethnicity, prejudice, and discrimination are of particular interest in this search (3). The department has an active and growing doctoral program in Systems Science/Psychology which encourages students to draw from many areas within psychology as well as from other disciplines.

Responsibilities for this position include productive research on applied psychological topics, teaching in areas of expertise at undergraduate and graduate levels, supervising dissertations and graduate practica, and participation in faculty governance. Qualifications include a doctoral degree in psychology and a commitment to conceptually based applied research, as demonstrated in dissertation or published research. Applied psychologists with scheduled completion dates for the dissertation are welcome to submit applications (4). Our university values campus diversity and demonstrates this in campus initiatives; we particularly encourage members of historically under-represented groups to apply (5).

Send letter of application, vita, statement of applied research interests and experiences, copies of papers, statement of teaching interests/ philosophy, statement of experience working with students of diverse backgrounds (6), and at least three letters of reference to Applied Psychology Search Committee, Department of Psychology-PSY, Portland State University. . . . Portland State University is an Affirmative Action/ Equal Opportunity Institution. www.psypdx.edu

Comments:

1. multiple levels and broad professional area
2. broadened academic areas to draw from
3. greater focus on research and teaching on cultural issues
4. call to young professionals
5. distinctive diversity invitation
6. specific emphasis on working with students from diverse backgrounds

a number of qualified candidates from under-represented groups (personal communication, 9-16-04).

We provide additional examples of actual ads from *The Chronicle of Higher Education* with commentary on how well they appeal to diverse constituents on pages 16–18.

What if your department or college does not have diversity initiatives that can be mentioned in position listings? Obviously, you can't make something up, just paying lip service to the diversity mantra. On the other hand, you may gauge your institution's commitment to diversity and its openness to attract applicants from traditionally underrepresented groups in your consultations with stakeholders, conversations with the hiring authority, and the goals you establish for the search (see Chapter 1). Even if your diversity initiatives are only at the planning stage, consider mentioning plans for diversity initiatives at the department or institution level in your ads.

Test the allure of the ads you develop by asking key constituents to read and comment on them. To test the legality of your advertisement (compliance with EEO/AA regulations), ask your Human Resources department or Diversity Office to review it. For high-level positions, review by the institution's legal counsel may be appropriate. Not only is it important to avert discrimination; it is vital if you intentionally seek to attract a diverse and representative applicant pool.

Securing Approval

Before the position is opened, both the position description and profile need to be approved. To do this, we like to invite the person who charged the committee to a committee meeting. We begin with a review of the breadth of our research, our findings and assumptions, and we explain the decisions we made about the priorities we saw. This sets the stage for sharing the committee's vision of the position and the ideal candidate. Remember, search committees can add significant value to the department and the institution by illuminating the vision and prospective scope of the position. Sometimes "outsiders" uncover the hidden agendas and festering issues; sometimes they can see with "beginners' eyes" the potential offered by the opening. The bottom line is: no approval, no search.

It is critical that you do not inadvertently discriminate against applicants on the basis of gender, race, age, religion, national origin, citizenship, or physical ability. By including your Human Resources department or Diversity Office, and perhaps even your institution's legal counsel in the approval process, you can be confident that the legal aspects of the position will be appropriately addressed. Ask them to review the final job description to ensure that it complies with government regulations and the ethical principles of the institution.

Potential Pitfalls

- **"We'll know the good applicants when we see them."** Indistinct criteria and lack of consensus about the position requirements lead to unimaginative advertising, homogeneous applicant pools, and biased or aborted processes. The committee cannot assume that consensus will be reached without rigorous dialogue up front.
- **The tendency to confuse the function of the office with the qualifications of the position.** Job descriptions that obfuscate what is required of the person and what is expected of the department attract ill-suited applicants, waste the time of the committee and the applicants, and prolong the search.
- **Establishing requirements that are too restrictive or unrealistic, thus reducing the applicant pool.** We believe that the purpose of the search committee is to attract a large, *qualified* applicant pool from which candidates with varying strengths can be chosen.
- **Organizational, leadership, or deep-rooted perceptual biases surface during your fact-finding activities.** You may uncover an entrenched structural problem that may make the position unattractive to prospective candidates or encumber its evolution. Once discovered, these issues must be disclosed and resolved before the search is opened. We believe it is the search committee's ethical responsibility to the institution to address them for the sake of both the institution and the prospective candidates.

Checklist for Profile and Position Description

- ❒ Researched the current responsibilities and emerging needs of the position
- ❒ Consulted the key stakeholders for their input
- ❒ Created the position description
- ❒ Created the profile
- ❒ Tested the appeal of the position description
- ❒ Created the announcement for the position as it will actually appear in advertisements
- ❒ Consulted with human resources, diversity office, legal counsel as appropriate
- ❒ Secured approvals for the advertisement

Ad Examples from actual listings in *The Chronicle of Higher Education*

Example of Long vs. Short Ads for the Same Position

Long advertisement

BIOLOGY
Assistant Professor, Tenure Track

The Department of Biology at [redacted] invites applications for a tenure-track position at the assistant professor level in some aspect of genomic biology. Areas of interest include, but are not limited to, comparative or functional genomics, protein structure and interactions, and metabolic relations. We especially desire candidates having an experimental research program that can involve undergraduate biology majors. Teaching duties include participation in a team-taught, introductory course that covers genetics, cellular, and molecular biology and includes a lab component, and two upper-level courses in the candidate's area, one with lab. A Ph.D. in biological sciences is required, and postdoctoral experience is expected. Send curriculum vitae and a statement of research and teaching interests to Genomic Biologist Search Committee, Department of Biology, P.O. Box 5000, [redacted]. Have three letters of recommendation sent separately.

Review of applications will begin October 18, 2004, and continue until the position is filled. Further information on the department can be found at [redacted].

Short advertisement

BIOLOGY
Assistant Professor, Tenure Track

The Department of Biology at [redacted] invites applications for a tenure-track position at the assistant professor level in some aspect of genomic biology. Details about the position, the College, and the application procedure may be found on our website: http:///www.*******.edu/~biology.

Diversity Critique of Actual Ads from *The Chronicle of Higher Education*

This listing provides the basic requirements for the candidate. However, beyond the mandatory AA/EOE listing, there is nothing to make this attractive to candidates from underrepresented groups.

SOUTH ASIAN HISTORY: The ████ University History Department invites applications for a tenure-track assistant professorship in modern South Asian history to begin July 1, 2005. Teaching expectations include colonial and post-independence South Asian history. Applicants must have their Ph.D. by Fall 2005. Evidence of scholarly potential and of a strong commitment to teaching expected. ████ is an AA/EOE. Please send letter of application, CV, and three letters of reference to Professor R.Laurence Moore, ████ University, Department of History, McGraw Hall, ████ (e-mail: ████) Application deadline is October 15, 2004.

The following ad is a small improvement, as it gives more information about the college's setting, the nature of the position and the diverse student population.

East Asian History Faculty

████ University enrolls approximately 9,000 students in graduate and undergraduate programs. The University is located in the borough of ████ in a charming rural setting and is within 20 minutes driving time of the diverse metropolitan areas ████. The University is very interested in hiring employees who have had extensive experience with diverse populations.

████ University invites applications for a full-time, tenure-track position to teach East Asian history with a secondary field in Europe (including Russia), or South Asia, or Africa, beginning in August 2005. Applicants must demonstrate preparation in the primary and secondary fields, and an ability and willingness to teach one or both of ████ University's History of Civilization courses. The teaching load is 12 s.h. each semester. ABD required; Ph.D. must be conferred by the beginning of the second year of appointment. Evidence of college teaching excellence, a commitment to research and a successful interview are also required. Send letter of application, vita, official graduate and undergraduate transcripts, and three current letters of recommendation to: East Asian Search Committee, Department of History, ████. Review of applications will begin October 1 and continue until the position is filled.

For full description, criteria and complete listing of vacancies visit our Web site at ████

████ University is an AA/EOE member of the PA State System of Higher Education and actively solicits applications from women and minorities.

(continued)

(continued)

The following ad provides the most information and leeway in terms of recruiting for diversity. The strength of this listing is its complete information about the position, the program, and also diversity initiatives that are currently in place and more that are being planned. There is flexibility in the announcement which leaves the door open to attract applicants from diverse backgrounds. Its final statement on commitment to diverse applicants is also stronger than the statements found in the other two ads.

Department of Communication
College of Arts and Sciences
University [redacted]

The University of [redacted] seeks a tenure-track assistant professor in the area of race/ethnicity and communication in the Department of Communication. Our graduate and undergraduate programs are founded on the principles of intellectual and cultural pluralism, interdisciplinary theorizing, diverse methods of inquiry, public scholarship and community engagement, and innovation through collaboration among faculty and students. Building upon these core principles, Department faculty have identified seven areas of emphasis—communication and culture; international communication; political communication; rhetoric and critical studies; social interaction; technology and society; and journalism. New faculty are expected to contribute significantly to at least one of these areas.

Candidates should have interests in race/ethnicity and communication, defined broadly to include face-to-face, on-line, mediated, or mass-mediated contexts. Particular focus may include critical race theory; the social construction of race in relationship to issues of power; the shifting nature of conceptualizations of race; the enactment or challenging of racial conceptions through media representations, public discourse, or rhetoric; the ways in which cultural ideologies are constructed by, are reflective of, and/or contribute to communication about race; transnational or postcolonial analyses of race; anti-racist inter-cultural discourses; linkages among race and other 'differences' such as gender or class; racialization, nationalism and diaspora; or the creation of identity (e.g., political, social) within groups that have been historically marginalized.

The Department of Communication has plans for an interdisciplinary center on communication and issues of difference; our new colleague will play a central part in shaping that initiative. The Department of Communication was recognized in 2002–2003 as a campus leader in the retention of under-represented minority students and includes several faculty who are involved in diversity-related research, teaching, and service. The University of [redacted] has a substantial institutional commitment to these issues.

Faculty are expected to conduct research, teach four courses during a three-quarter academic year, and supervise graduate students at the master's and doctoral levels. Applicants must demonstrate a potential for excellence in research and teaching and the ability to contribute to the Department's curriculum. Experience mentoring students of under-represented groups would be highly valued. Candidates must have earned or be close to completion of a Ph.D. by September 2005, in a field related to the positions offered. Candidates should send a letter of application, curriculum vitae, statement of research and teaching interests, copies of teaching evaluations, and three letters of recommendation.

The start date for this position is September 16, 2005. Applications will be reviewed beginning October 15, 2004, and until the positions are filled. Send application material to: [redacted]

The University of [redacted] is the largest and most active research institution in the northwest with several extensive libraries and substantial computing and support facilities. The Department of Communication is committed to building a culturally diverse faculty and strongly encourages applications from women, minorities, individuals with disabilities, and covered veterans. The University of [redacted] is an affirmative action, equal opportunity employer.

References

Faculty Recruitment Handbook, NSF Advance at the University of Michigan Academic Year 2004—2005. Retrieved 02/24/05 from www.umich.edu/~advproj/handbook.pdf

Faculty Search Committee Guidelines (2004–2005) Advertising the Position, Advertising Wording. Retrieved 02/25/05 from www.cwru.edu/president/aaction/guide.html#wording

University of Maryland Diversity Database. *Moving toward Community, Procedures and Guidelines for Conducting Faculty and Staff Searches at UMCP,* Chapter 1, Developing a Position Description (September, 1999). Retrieved 02/24/05 from www.inform.umd.edu/EdRes/Topic/Diversity/Response/UM/Proc/chap1.html

CHAPTER 3

Recruiting Candidates

In this chapter, you will

- Determine the best resources for reaching and attracting top candidates
- Choose the most judicious use of limited advertising dollars
- Devise inventive ways of spreading the word about your opening
- Use networking and other targeted techniques to recruit a diverse pool of qualified candidates

Getting Started

NOW THAT YOUR AD is written, you're probably feeling the momentum building. Like most search committees, you want to get moving on the advertising and promotion of the position. Typically search committees initiate their promotion with tried and true sources like *The Chronicle of Higher Education*, newsletters of selected professional organizations, and the college's web site. We do, too! However, using *only* the channels that have always been used will likely attract a small, homogeneous applicant pool. Now is the time to consider additional channels that are likely to yield a larger, more diverse group of applicants.

Choosing Where to Advertise

The key to placing announcements strategically is to think like the candidates you want to attract. Where are they likely to be looking for premium opportunities? Because your ideal candidate may not be looking for a new position, brainstorm with the committee, "What are the media—print and electronic—and networking connections that our ideal candidate would typically access?" Does your profile suggest skill sets that might lead you to more specialized niche media? To attract diversity candidates, seek out media and networks like professional associations, clubs, and fraternal organizations that appeal to the cultural interests of traditionally underrepresented groups.

Certain journals and publications like *The Chronicle of Higher Education* are "a must" for placing mid- and high-level academic and administrative postings. Most can be accessed electronically, an increasingly popular method used by applicants. However, if you want to attract a diverse candidate pool, don't rely on just a standard listing in *The Chronicle*. One psychology department chair from a New York university told us that a search committee he commissioned believed that a posting in the *The Chronicle* with the EEO/AA tag line would attract all the eligible applicants. They were distressed when not one of their applicants was from a minority group. This is worth repeating: To attract a diverse applicant pool, you must consider diverse venues for your position announcement.

In addition to the general academic listing, most professional organizations have newsletters and websites that include job listings. These are another good way to increase the diversity of your applicant pool. Some examples include

- American Association of University Women (AAUW.org)
- Black Issues in Higher Education (black issues.com)

- Society of Women Engineers (swe.org)
- Abilities! (ncds.org)
- National Association of Asian American Professionals (naap.org)
- American Disability Association (adanet.org)
- American Indian Science and Engineering Society (aises.org)
- Minority & Women Doctoral Directory (mwdd.com)
- Latino Link (latinolink.com)
- Advancing Women (advancingwomen.com)
- DiversiLink (diversilink.com)
- Hispanic Online (hisp.com)
- Hispanic Outlook in Higher Education
- University Faculty Voice (distributed to faculty in Historically Black Colleges and Universities)
- The National Association of Hispanic Journalists (nahj.org)
- AALANA recruitment resources (rit.edu)

The offices of Human Resources, the Dean, or Diversity/Equal Opportunity may have additional recommendations for sourcing diversity candidates based on their experience from prior searches. They are also likely to be rich resources for refining, costing, and placing print and electronic ads.

The Myths of the Diversity Candidate

Howard's Story

Some academic fields are still characterized by an oversupply of available professors. As a new Harvard-educated academic with a Ph.D. in history, I felt fortunate to find a position, any position, even though it was a one-year visiting assistant professorship in a small Northeastern college. I also felt fortunate a year later to land a tenure-track position at a larger Western university. It wasn't easy being an African American in an overwhelmingly white student/faculty environment, but I turned the experience into an opportunity by writing a conference paper on teaching genocide to a homogeneous population. Shortly after receiving tenure, I again began a job search to move back east, primarily to be closer to my aging parents. Still, the market was crowded with applicants, and schools could precisely fill their teaching niches with the person they wanted. When I was offered the position at a comprehensive liberal arts college in upstate New York, I felt lucky to have landed the position. Through all of my job searches, I never felt that I was specifically recruited as a faculty of color. My job search was conducted solely through my professional organization, and I was never specifically targeted for special consideration as a diversity candidate with a Ph.D. from a prestigious institution. When I arrived in my new home town, I became acculturated to the area primarily on my own, through friends of friends.

Would you be surprised to learn that Howard's experience is typical? Diversity expert Daryl Smith studied a group of 393 white and minority Ph.D.s who were recipients of prestigious fellowships. Her findings challenge some commonly held myths about diversity candidates in academia, including the following:

Myth: Because there are so few faculty of color, they are sought by numerous institutions that compete in the hiring process for these candidates.

Reality: While some minority candidates had more than one offer, none found bidding wars to be their experience.

Myth: The scarcity of faculty of color in the sciences means that few are available and those who are available are in high demand.

Reality: Most scientists in Smith's study went on to postdoctoral work and were quite concerned about finding academic positions.

Myth: Candidates from prestigious institutions are interested in being considered by only the most prestigious institutions, making it virtually impossible for other institutions to recruit them.

Reality: Candidates expressed an interest in a wide variety of positions.

Smith concludes that, for institutions looking to diversify their faculty, there are candidates available to consider their positions. But what are the most successful ways to attract diversity candidates?

In a survey of 451 journalism and mass communication programs, Lee Becker and his colleagues at the University of Georgia were able to identify three programs that had substantially increased their female and minority hiring over the previous decade—the University of Alabama, the University of Florida, and the University of Missouri. They conducted detailed interviews at each institution and found some common threads in their approach to increasing diversity in the faculty. Becker and his colleagues drew the following conclusions from their studies:

- Administrators need to use their bully pulpits. Diversification requires strong leadership.
- Targeted hiring works. If it is available, use it.
- Be flexible in job descriptions. Specificity works against diversification.
- Diversify the curriculum. Use curricular inclusiveness to recruit.
- Network early—even if there isn't an opening. It will pay dividends later.
- Be creative in finding ways to promote the community. Focus on housing, schools, churches, and cultural offerings.
- Get undergraduates interested in careers as professors. A diverse pool of doctoral students is crucial to faculty diversification.
- Mentor female and minority faculty carefully. Retention is essential to increase diversification.
- Use the diversity of the students as a selling point. Faculty want to work with students like themselves.

At the same time, the researchers acknowledged that large departments and schools with many faculty positions enjoyed more flexibility in their hiring, because they did not have to fill narrow teaching slots. Smaller schools and programs may not enjoy such hiring flexibility to support their diversity efforts. This assertion is further supported by many of our book's Examples Worth Noting, which overwhelmingly come from larger institutions.

Research consistently shows that personal networking is the single most important strategy to diversify your applicant pool. In the following sections, we offer suggestions for developing a referral network to diversify your applicant pool.

Recruiting Beyond the Classifieds and Databases

Robert's Story

A few years ago, I led the search committee for the Vice President of Student Development at a Midwest liberal arts college. Among the strategies for widening the scope of advertising was sending a personal note and a copy of the announcement to college presidents and academic colleagues from schools like ours. In the note, we asked for their assistance in identifying prime diversity applicants, and we guaranteed that any applicant they personally referred would be interviewed. We received ten personal referrals; half were diversity candidates (women and people of color). We interviewed all of them. One of the candidates was referred by two and another by three external colleagues. We knew immediately that they were exceptional candidates and, in fact, they both became finalists. Without knowing the sources of the referrals, the president chose the minority candidate who had been referred by three external colleagues.

The best way to attract high-caliber candidates is to engage the personal and on-line professional networks of each of your committee members and other interested constituents. Here are some of the ways you can do that:

- Share information about the opening with senior leaders and incumbents from similar institutions as well as colleagues in schools and academic disciplines who interact with talented people who might be prospects. Specifically request personal referrals of candidates they believe are outstanding. It helps to indicate that their referrals will receive immediate and personal attention in the process. Blanketing mailing lists with position announcements is rarely successful, but targeted networking can often yield fruitful results.
- Send announcements and supporting documents to professional associations, honor societies, journal editors, and conference leaders in the field where the opening occurs.
- Ask on-line forums to post your opening for members.
- Contact institutions that have recently searched for or successfully hired for a similar position. They may reveal new sources of candidates; they may even refer a finalist whom they did not select.
- Women's colleges and historically Black and Hispanic colleges and universities can be contacted for alumni information and leads on potential candidates. All efforts to recruit minority and female candidates should be noted

for the record and shared with future search committees.

- The University of Maryland also recommends recruiting at conferences that target minority professionals, making the excellent point that your presence at such events means more than a letter or email.

In light of recent litigation regarding specific student recruiting targeted to race, and the variability of these laws from state to state, Jonathan Alger, Vice Provost and General Legal Counsel at Rutgers University, advises search committees that consider adopting these or similar practices to consult with their legal counsel. Likewise, any informal offer agreement should be

Examples Worth Noting: Expanding the Diversity of a Candidate Pool

Rochester Institute of Technology in Rochester, New York won national attention and citation in *Black Issues in Higher Education* for its programs that have successfully recruited new faculty from underrepresented groups. By personal invitation of the President, outstanding doctoral candidates from underrepresented groups are hosted on campus for a weekend program known as "Future Faculty Career Exploration Program" where they are courted by respective academic departments. Representation of minority faculty has increased by 30 percent for two consecutive years as a result.

Several years ago, the **University of Mississippi** School of Education had found it difficult to attract even one black faculty member for six faculty openings, despite national searches for each position. Rallied to action, all six search committees convened a strategy mega-meeting to invent a way to recruit minority talent. Using a best-in-class approach adapted from quality management principles, they consulted with an athletic coach at the university whose success in recruiting minority talent was legendary and an army recruiter with an excellent record of recruiting African Americans.

Here's what they did that made the difference:

1. The search committees agreed to recruit as a single entity.
2. They set recruiting targets and committed as a whole to meeting them.
3. They called minority alumni and asked if they knew of any qualified African American who would be interested in and qualified for any of the six positions, or a contact who might know qualified candidates.
4. They phoned every lead they received from the alumni and screened them for their interest and qualifications.
5. Each viable candidate was personally invited by the dean to visit the campus.
6. The person referring the candidate who accepted the campus visit invitation was notified and engaged in the recruitment process. They were asked, "What would it take for us to secure this candidate?"
7. The dean personally extended offers to the candidates selected by the search committee. Informal written agreements at the time of the offer established a foundation of commitment on the part of both parties.
8. Candidates were called within a few days to finalize the terms of the offer, and in most cases, a formal contract was offered.

What were the results? The School identified nine highly talented candidates. Seven visited the campus and completed the interview process. Four were offered appointments and three accepted.

drawn up with prior consultation with legal counsel or Human Resources. A written agreement may in some instances be construed as a binding contract (personal communication 11-18-04).

The point is *inclusion*. Casting a wide net from the very beginning, to attract a full and inclusive range of candidates, makes it more likely that race, gender, sexual orientation, disability, or ethnicity will not be a deciding factor at the conclusion of the search. By exercising this level of flexibility, search committees can avert potential legal pitfalls (Alger, personal communication, 2-28-05).

Potential Pitfalls

- **Posting the position using the same sources that you've always used.** Diversifying the sources and activating contacts through networking with colleagues expand the reach of your opening and increase the possibility of attracting diverse and differently talented, highly qualified candidates with little increase in cost.
- **Putting all your advertising dollars into one or two resources.** Expand into other media. They may cost relatively little in comparison to the payoff in the applicant pool.
- **Exhibiting neutrality or indifference regarding diversity.** People of color will be the majority in the United States by 2050. Further, the student body is becoming increasingly diverse at a much faster rate than the faculty who teach them. It is crucial for academic institutions to prepare for this dramatic demographic shift by attracting faculty and administrators who better represent the diversity of the future student body.

CHECKLIST FOR RECRUITING CANDIDATES

- ❒ Researched and chose the print and electronic venues to place the ad
- ❒ Considered alternative approaches to recruiting qualified candidates
- ❒ Determined the need to consult with legal counsel and Human Resources
- ❒ Planned and delegated targeted networking to recruit diversity candidates
- ❒ Activated various networks to spread the word
    - Network: *The Chronicle of Higher Education*
    - Network: Professional trade associations
    - Network: Websites of interest to the field
    - Network: Personal contacts
    - Network: Other

References

Becker, L. B., Punathambekar, A., & Huh, J. (2001). *Evaluating the outcomes of diversification initiatives: Stability and change in journalism and mass communication faculties 1989–1998.* Athens, GA: The Cox Center. May be retrieved from www.grady.uga.edu/annualsurveys/facultydiversity/knightsummary.htm

Hamilton, K. (2003). Mission Possible. *Black Issues in Higher Education, 20* (18), 24–27.

Payne, J., & Blackbourn, J. M. (1994). Using best of class concepts to improve recruitment. *The Journal for Quality and Participation, 17* (1), 76–81.

Smith, D. G. (1996). *Achieving faculty diversity: Debunking the myths.* Washington, DC: Association of American Colleges and Universities

University of Maryland Diversity Database: *Moving toward Community, Procedures and Guidelines for Conducting Faculty and Staff Searches at UMCP*, Chapter 3, Developing Search and Screening Procedures (September, 1999). Retrieved 02/24/05 from www.inform.umd.edu/EdRes/Topic/Diversity/Response/UM/Proc/chap3.html

CHAPTER 4

Evaluating Resumés

In this chapter, you will

- Acknowledge and track each application for the position as it arrives
- Use the position description and profile to set up an evaluation framework for screening resumés
- Determine the best way for the committee to work on initial screenings
- Identify techniques to screen for diversity candidates
- Begin your first contact with applicants, rejecting those who do not meet your criteria

Getting Started

YOU HAVE REACHED your first milestone—a respectable applicant pool. You're probably feeling excited and somewhat curious about who applied. At this point it's time to acknowledge the applicants, review resumés, rate applicants, and choose the candidates. As a committee, you have a number of decisions to make about the method you'll use to screen the resumés, the criteria you'll employ to rate the applicants, and the dialogue process you'll implement to determine which candidates to pursue. Strategic leadership from the committee chair is key in guiding the dialogue process of the initial meeting to reach consensus on the candidates.

Acknowledging the Applicants

Each application for the position should be acknowledged as soon as it arrives. Have you decided who will receive and track the applications? In some schools, Human Resources prefers to receive applications for all positions so they can track statistics institution-wide. Some search committees choose to have the applications sent directly to the chair or to a designated person such as an administrative assistant. Each applicant's name, contact information, and date of application need to be entered on the tracking form. It also helps to include the source where the applicant learned of the position, if known, because this data allows you to evaluate your advertising and networking effectiveness.

The acknowledgement to the applicant, often sent via e-mail or postcard by your Human Resources office, should be kept simple. Page 28 shows a typical message to the candidate developed by the Human Resources Office at St. John Fisher College

Deciding on the Criteria for Evaluating Candidates

Before anyone on the search committee looks at even one resumé, you must agree on the criteria to be used for evaluation. This should be relatively easy, given the work that you put into defining the position, as described in Chapter 2. However, now is the time to operationalize the position description and profile; in other words, put into evaluative form the criteria by which you will judge your applicants. It does not have to be very detailed, but you should include the major features—the critical dimensions—of the position you advertised and against which you will evaluate each applicant.

An example of an initial screening form that was

DATE

NAME
ADDRESS
CITY/STATE/ZIP

Dear CANDIDATE,

Thank you for applying for the position of TITLE at St. John Fisher College. Your interest in the College is greatly appreciated.

The qualifications of each candidate will be reviewed carefully and compared with the position requirements for TITLE. You will be contacted if there is an interest in further discussions. Please be advised that your information will remain on file for one year. If you should have any specific questions in regard to our timeline and process, please feel free to contact us.

Best Regards,

Human Resources Office
St. John Fisher College
3690 East Avenue
Rochester, New York 14618
Phone: 585-385-8048
Fax: 585-385-2102
HR@SJFC.edu

used for a faculty position in television production appears on page 29.

Examples of two other initial screening forms that were used in actual searches appear at the end of this chapter.

Reviewing Resumés

The committee will be most successful if it follows this three-step approach to reviewing resumés:

Step 1: Individually, screen candidates.
Each committee member should first read every applicant's resumé and cover letter, without consulting others on the committee. Each of you was chosen to lend a specific expertise and perspective to the process. Screening on your own allows individual insights to be noted and reduces the tendency to go along with the majority view. This is especially valuable when you intend to generate an inclusive candidate pool. Using an initial screening form that contains both numerical weightings and qualitative comments on evidence enables you to clarify and codify your perceptions of each applicant. Not only will you be prepared for the initial screening meeting, you will be less likely to be sidetracked and better able to argue with evidence for the applicants you feel are most qualified for the position.

You might be able to expedite this step of the process before actually meeting, saving time and resources, by

Initial Screening Evaluation Form—blank form

Candidate Name: ______________________________

1. Evaluation of Academic Degrees
   Ph.D. 5——4——3——2——1 M.F.A.
   Comment on evidence that led to this rating:

2. Teaching Experience
   Extensive 5——4——3——2——1 no teaching experience
   Comment on evidence that led to this rating:

3. Scholarship
   Extensive 5——4——3——2——1 no scholarship
   Comment on evidence that led to this rating:

4. Ability to advise the TV Club
   Excellent 5——4——3——2——1 Poor
   Comment on evidence that led to this rating:

5. Ability to do academic advising for majors
   Excellent 5——4——3——2——1 Poor
   Comment on evidence that led to this rating:

6. Fit for the Department, Program, College
   Excellent 5——4——3——2——1 Poor
   Comment on evidence that led to this rating:

7. Familiarity with software, particularly Final Cut Pro.
   Excellent 5——4——3——2——1 Poor
   Comment on evidence that led to this rating:

8. Other comments:

Candidate Score: ———

Should we interview this candidate? ——yes —— no —— unsure

____
Reviewer

using a secure web site where resumés are posted. Committee members may indicate those applicants who are not qualified for the position and won't be pursued. In our experience, each search generates at least a few clearly unqualified applicants who would fall into this category. For example, a few years ago we had some Kodak retirees with no academic experience apply for a Vice President for Academic Affairs position. Clearly, they had no idea what such a position entailed! Other examples include the non-baccalaureate applicants for faculty positions and applicants who send handwritten resumés. However, the vast majority of applicants will be reviewed in the initial screening meeting after everyone on the committee has completed the individual evaluations.

An example of a completed initial screening form for a television production applicant appears on page 31.

Step 2: Compare rankings in a committee meeting.

Only after Step 1 has been completed should the committee meet to discuss the applicants. The purpose of this meeting is to define a reasonably sized, high-potential candidate pool to pursue. The chair should request that the committee members reserve sufficient time for the meeting to responsibly review each applicant. In a search with many applications to review, this meeting may take two hours or more.

The leadership of the chair is important for setting the appropriate tone, direction, and process for productive deliberation at this meeting. The meeting should open with a review of the profile and position description, the charge to the committee, and the goal of the meeting, which might sound like this:

The goal of today's meeting is to conduct a thorough dialogue about each of the applicants, carefully and fully consider the relevant evidence on each of them, and reach consensus about the best candidates to pursue.

Depending on the size of your applicant pool, an easy first round discussion could focus on which applicants to eliminate. You might begin by using the numbers—those applicants who didn't even make it onto your radar screen. When members concur that an applicant is inappropriate or totally unacceptable for the position, that applicant should be eliminated. For example, an applicant with *only* a B.S. in chemistry should be rejected on the first round for an assistant professor of biochemistry position.

Next, since all applicants must be accounted for, record the outcome of the decisions on the applicant tracking form you instituted. We find it helps to display the name, gender, race/ethnicity, and disposition sections of the tracking form using chart paper or projecting it on a screen so it is visible to all committee members. You'll need a scribe to record your decisions about applicants to be eliminated and the reasons, those to be immediately pursued, and those to be placed on hold.

When these details are resolved, the chair should review your prior dialogue about consensus and your agreements, and remind the committee of the importance of reaching a shared, acceptable decision on the candidates to pursue. Next, the committee needs to decide on an order of discussion, which could be done in a number of ways. One effective method, described previously, is to ask for a quick ranking of the applicants, based on the pre-meeting prioritization. As the rankings done by each committee member are written on the grid, you can immediately identify the unqualified applicants. Discussing the least desirable applicants first saves precious time and focuses your attention on those who are the most attractive. Even for the least favorite applicant, members must present their reasons for ranking and evaluation. The scribe tracks the key points on the ranking grid. Dialogue until consensus is reached.

Step 3: Identify top candidates.

If you have a large applicant pool, you need to decide how many to move to the next step in the process and how many to put on hold. Highly attractive candidates—the people you will seriously consider—will rise to the top of your rankings. Remember to record your decision for each applicant on the tracking form. At this point, members' unique perspectives fulfill a vital role. The richness of the candidate pool hinges on your insights and observations about the applicants' qualifications and your willingness to advocate for those you believe are the best fit for the position. Cite the evidence where their experience matches or complements both the profile and position description.

Initial Screening Evaluation Form—Sample Individual Evaluation

Candidate Name: *Stan Wellback*

1. Evaluation of Academic Degrees

   Ph.D. 5 4 (3) 2 1 M.F.A.

   Comment on evidence that led to this rating:

   I gave the candidate a 3 because he is ABD and may not complete the dissertation for another year.

2. Teaching Experience

   Extensive 5 4 (3) 2 1 no teaching experience

   Comment on evidence that led to this rating:

   I gave the candidate a 3 for three years teaching as an adjunct at the local community college.

3. Scholarship

   Extensive 5 (4) 3 2 1 no scholarship

   Comment on evidence that led to this rating:

   Candidate has two refereed papers and three conference presentations—very good for a doctoral candidate, shows a good habit of scholarship being pursued: 4

4. Ability to advise the TV Club

   Excellent 5 (4) 3 2 1 Poor

   Comment on evidence that led to this rating:

   Has served as teaching assistant in charge of TV studio, worked on newscast as an undergrad, did some work for local public access station—probably 4.

5. Ability to do academic advising for majors

   Excellent 5 4 3 (2) 1 Poor

   Comment on evidence that led to this rating:

   Probably can do it with a lot of mentoring: 2

6. Fit for the Department, Program, College

   Excellent 5 4 (3) 2 1 Poor

   Comment on evidence that led to this rating:

   Candidate may find it hard to come to a small college after graduate school at a major research university. However, good commitment to liberal arts and writing skills: 3

7. Familiarity with software, particularly Final Cut Pro.

   Excellent 5 4 (3) 2 1 Poor

   Comment on evidence that led to this rating:

   Candidate has used Final Cut Pro to produce several works during graduate school. Can use it, but has not taught it yet: 3.

   Other comments:

   Candidate is familiar with area from time as undergraduate at University of Rochester—this is good, winters won't be a shock. I am just afraid he won't consider us seriously if he has interviews at bigger programs.

   Candidate Score: 21

   Should we interview this candidate? X yes ____ no ____ unsure

   Roger Houston

   Reviewer

Identifying Diversity Candidates

Traditionally underrepresented groups are often eliminated in the initial screening process. This is particularly likely when a committee relies only on numerical rankings for their decisions. Contextualizing the job description and the profile expands your conversation about how a candidate could demonstrate the desired attributes, satisfy the experience qualifications, and meet the requirements of the position. It puts you on the alert for evidence of activity and contributions in areas outside your known or acknowledged spheres. The conversation may also reveal salient issues that affect your ability to attract a diverse candidate pool which may, in turn, necessitate your reconsideration of some of the criteria.

To illustrate, Turner notes that scholars of color and women may take different routes to the professoriate than majority scholars. Search committees would be wise to include in their initial pool candidates who have distinguished themselves in business, industry, community agencies, government, and the military, as well as traditional settings. As a case in point, the former mayor of Rochester, New York, a prominent African American, was recently appointed to a tenured faculty position in urban policy at the Rochester Institute of Technology. Intentionally looking for evidence such as membership in minority professional associations or scholarship in gender studies are ways to identify diversity candidates.

At the same time, search committees need to be mindful of recent legal scrutiny of programs recruiting only for faculty from traditionally underrepresented groups. Karen DePauw, Vice Provost for Graduate Studies and Dean of the Graduate School at Virginia Tech, advises that the search process must be "open"; that is, race may be used in consideration of a candidate, but a candidate cannot be eliminated solely on the basis of race or gender (i.e., non-minority candidates must also be considered). While the impetus for diversity hiring must come from the person who charged the committee, the search committee should still be open to consider *all* applicants, including those whose professional profile diverges from that of the traditional applicant pool (personal communication, 01-27-05).

Eliminating Unqualified Applicants

After the preliminary screening, notify those applicants you will not be pursuing further. Rejection letters should be short, respectful, and straightforward. Even though the application may have been e-mailed, we recommend that the letter be sent via hard copy to the applicant's home address. Two sample rejection letters appear on page 33.

Potential Pitfalls

- **Failure to use a systematic process.** This is often the biggest obstacle to successfully screening resumés. A number of search committee chairs have told us, "We will know the best candidates when we see the resumés." Such an attitude presumes that everyone on the search committee shares exactly the same perceptions about the position and the applicants. Clearly, this is impossible. While you have carefully defined the parameters of your search using the guidelines in Chapter 2, there are many areas open for discussion and interpretation. For example, an applicant for a dean's position may appeal to some members on the basis of pedigree, to others on the basis of experience, and to still others on the basis of scholarship. While all are important qualifications for an academic administrator, the search committee will need to hash out the relative importance of each.
- **Pressure to conform to the majority perspective**. Search committee members may feel pressure (real or imagined) to conform to the opinions of others, especially members with higher status. We know from group dynamics literature that groups always pressure their members to conform to the majority opinion. However, we also know that the most successful groups encourage the sharing of divergent opinions to ensure that the group has considered all sides of an issue. The search committee chair has an obligation to create a climate of trust and mutual respect so that all opinions may be heard, regardless of the opinions of the higher status members.

Sample Rejection Letters

Sample 1

Dear Dr. Gregg:

Thank you for your application for the faculty position in digital television production at St. John Fisher College.

We received a number of applications for this position and reviewed each applicant's qualifications carefully, and your background represents some highly desirable characteristics. However, we regret to inform you that we will not be pursuing your application further.

Thank you for your interest, and we wish you success with your future career plans.

Sincerely,

Barbara Seville, Chair
Search Committee

Sample 2

Dear Dr. Shafiq:

Thank you for your interest in the Registrar position in the College of Arts and Sciences at the University of Rochester. The Search Committee has carefully reviewed your experience and background against our criteria. While your credentials and experience represent significant accomplishments, we found the qualifications of other applicants more closely fit our needs. We will not be considering your application further.

We wish you much success in your career search and thank you for your interest in the University of Rochester.

Sincerely,

Naomi Winter, Chair
Search Committee

Checklist for Evaluating Resumés

- ❒ Acknowledged each application as it arrived and entered information onto tracking form
- ❒ Developed preliminary evaluation form
- ❒ Screened applicants individually
- ❒ Discussed rankings and evidence
- ❒ Carefully screened for diversity applicants
- ❒ Identified applicants to pursue, reject, and put on hold
- ❒ Noted all decisions on the tracking sheet
- ❒ Sent rejection letters to those who will not be continuing in the process

Sample Evaluation Forms

A sample evaluation form (example 1) used in a recent search for a professor in education appears on page 35.

In a recent administrative search at a medical school, the committee did initial screening using the form that appears on page 36 (example 2).

Reference

Turner, C. S. (2002). *Diversifying the faculty: A guidebook for search committees.* Washington, DC: Association of American Colleges and Universities, p. 21.

Example 1

CREDENTIAL RATING SHEET

Education Department Search

Candidate: ______________________

Evaluator: ______________________

Position applying for:
Childhood: ________
Special Ed: ________
Adolescence: ________

After reviewing the application letter, resumé, transcripts, and recommendations, please rate the following criteria on a scale of 1 to 5, with 5 high.

	Rating	Comments
1. Qualifications		
A. Ph.D./Ed.D./ABD	____	
B. Strength of Educational Background (Specializations and breadth)	____	
C. NYS Teaching Certification	____	
2. Scholarship/Scholarship Potential		
A. Publications	____	
B. Grants	____	
C. Academic Record/Transcripts	____	
D. Conferences/Presentations	____	
E. Awards and Honors	____	
3. Teaching Experience		
A. Public School Classroom (minimum 5 years)	____	
B. College	____	
C. Supervision of Pre-service Teachers	____	
D. Experience with Diverse Populations	____	
4. References (3)	____	
5. Professional Service & Community Involvement		
A. In-service Workshops/Consultant	____	
B. Service on Professional Boards or Committees	____	
C. Service on College/University Committees	____	
D. Organizational Membership/Conference Awards	____	
6. Other		
A. Skills in Computer Technology	____	
B. Oral and Written Skills	____	
TOTAL	____	

Example 2

ADMINISTRATIVE SCREENING FORM

Name of Applicant: ______________________________

Date Resumé Received: ______________________________

Name of Reviewer: ______________________________

Skills and Abilities	Has Skill	Lacks Skill	Doesn't Say
Organizational Development			
Budget Management			
Relationship Building			
Quality Improvement			
Communication at Multiple Levels			
Fundraising			
Grant Administration			
Regulatory Compliance			
Creation of a Team			
Health Care			

Education: ______________________________

Experience: ______________________________

Next step: ______ Interview ______ Letter—not a candidate ______ Letter—"Hold"

CHAPTER 5

Preparing to Interview

In this chapter, you will

- Understand the nature and function of an employment interview
- Consider the guidelines for asking effective questions in phone screens and in-person interviews
- Arrange for training the search committee
- Acquire an understanding of legal and illegal questions
- Develop behavioral event interview questions that get to the heart of your position's critical dimensions
- Prepare other campus constituencies to participate in the interview process

Getting Started

CONGRATULATIONS! Your preliminary screening of resumés is done and you are ready to contact the candidates you wish to pursue. You're probably planning to start with a phone screen or a meeting at an academic conference placement center to narrow down the candidate pool to those you will invite to campus for an on-site interview.

This is the step in the process where the search committee sharpens its interviewing skills. Committee members have undoubtedly come into the process with a wide range of interviewing experiences and skills. Some may have participated in many searches, while others may have participated only as the interviewee in their own hiring. It is important to ensure that committee members have a common perception of the interview process and agree on the nature and function of the questions you will ask. Additionally, you must be absolutely sure that no one on the committee will jeopardize the integrity of the search by asking illegal interview questions.

Interview Training

Consider conducting a focused training session on interviewing for the committee and the other constituencies who will meet the candidates. Expertise is probably readily available on campus through the Human Resources, Diversity, or Career Services offices, or an academic department such as Management or Communications. Topics should include structuring the interview, formulating questions, types of questions (closed vs. open), illegal questions, behavioral event interviewing, and interviewing techniques. Group training ensures that you are all on the same page when it comes to the interview process and reduces the likelihood that poor planning or illegal questions will derail your process or tarnish the reputation of the institution.

Let's investigate these topics in detail now.

The Nature of the Interview

An interview is a specialized form of interpersonal communication in which two (or more) individuals come together for a specific purpose with a set agenda. The format generally includes the asking and answering of questions.

Most people think about interviewing in terms of selection or employment interviews. But we use interviews in a number of other ways: to take surveys, to gather information for a news story, to evaluate a person's performance on the job, to counsel individuals, to persuade someone, and to gather medical information on a patient, to name just a few. While interviews can be valuable tools in many segments of our work and professional lives, they are not absolute or valid measures of a person's ability to perform a job. The employment interview seeks to uncover as much information as possible to determine if a candidate is a fit for the job. However, the interview is not foolproof and should not be the only factor considered when choosing your final candidate.

The Structure of the Interview

A good interview is like a story: it has an introduction, a body, and a conclusion. Skilled interviewers incorporate this structure in organizing their interviews because it optimizes their effectiveness and enhances the performance of the candidate.

Introduction

The essential elements of the introduction include greeting the candidate by name, shaking hands (if the interview is in person), and making the candidate feel comfortable. Your goal is to achieve rapport and orient the candidate to the interview process. Research reveals that you have achieved rapport when the candidate feels comfortable in the situation and understands the process.

Here is an example of an introduction for an interview for a college career counselor position:

Good morning, Mr. Abraham. I'm Tabita Rodriguez, Director of the Career Services Office. How are you today? (smiling and extending hand)

Fine, thank you. Please, call me David. *(handshake)*

Okay, David. And I prefer that you call me Tabita. May I take your coat? Did you have any trouble finding our office?

No, your directions were excellent. Parking seems to be a little difficult around here, though.

I know, if you don't arrive early, you have quite a walk to your office. Can I get you some coffee?

No thank you, but I would appreciate a glass of water.

I have some bottled water right here. (gives water) *Won't you have a seat?* (both take a seat) *Are you comfortable?*

Yes, thank you.

Let's get started. First I want to tell you about how we plan to proceed today. Your interview with me is the first step in the interview process. We will be together for about thirty to forty-five minutes. I'll ask you some questions from your resumé about your education and your past work experience. Then I'll tell you a little bit about the position here at the university. Finally, you'll have a chance to ask me any questions that you might have, and I'll conclude by talking about the next step in the process. How does that sound?

That sounds fine, Tabita.

In this introduction, Tabita made David feel welcomed and asked some general questions to make him feel comfortable in the setting. She also told him exactly how the interview would proceed so he could plan his strategy appropriately.

Body

In the body of the interview, you ask a variety of questions that cover the points you wish to explore with the candidate. In this early stage of interview planning it's very tempting to plunge into developing questions. Resist the temptation for a moment and attend to the plan for the interview. We recommend that you begin with an agenda. There are two important benefits to using an agenda. First, it gives the candidates a logical framework in which to present their qualifications in the best possible light. Second, using an organized agenda with each of your candidates makes it easier for you to compare them after the interviews in order to select your finalists.

Organize the agenda by listing the ideas and topics you want to cover with the candidate, beginning with the most important one first. For the preliminary screening interview with David above, the agenda might look something like this:

- *Education*
  - *Graduate*
  - *Undergraduate*
- *Work Experience*
  - *Career counseling: LeMoyne College*
  - *Residential life staff: Syracuse University*
- *Specific skills for the position*
  - *Counseling*
  - *Program development*
  - *Recruiting*
  - *Resumé writing*

- *Overview of the position*
- *Candidate questions*

Conclusion
The conclusion closes the interview. You express appreciation for the candidate's interest in your position and explain the next step in the selection process. The conclusion usually flows naturally from the last question that the candidate asks of the interviewer. Here is an example of a conclusion for the screening interview above:

David, if you have no more questions for me, I'd like to thank you for coming today and interviewing for our position. Here is my business card. Please feel free to call or e-mail if you have any further questions. We plan to be interviewing for this position through the end of next week, so it will probably be at least ten days before you hear from us. We will let you know by phone if you will be coming back for a second interview to meet the entire department team. Thank you again for your interest in the position.

Now that you have a good idea of the structure of the interview, you are ready to plan your specific questions.

Formulating Questions

Now that you have organized the agenda, you're ready to formulate the questions. As you begin, committee members may suggest commonly asked questions like these:

- Where do you want to be in five years?
- Do you consider yourself a people person?
- What's your opinion on . . . ?
- How would your best friend/worst enemy describe you?
- What would you do if . . . ?

As sensible as these may seem, they are ineffective in helping the search committee select the best candidate for the job. In order to craft questions that will elicit the candidates' qualifications, interest, and fit for the position, revisit each candidate's initial screening form. Because it is based on the profile and position description, it reminds you of the areas where the candidate's application information is incomplete. For each of these areas, formulate questions to elicit the additional information you want to know.

The next step is to convert the points raised by the committee into questions. The chart on page 40, developed by the search committee for an education department faculty opening, illustrates the process of formulating questions from the preliminary screening form.

Tips for Formulating Questions
Formulating questions is both an art and a science. The wording of the question has a significant impact on the quality of the answers you receive. Here are some tips gleaned from our research and experience:

- **Limit closed questions**: Closed questions elicit a single reply or yes/no response, for example. "Did you do curriculum development?" or "What courses did you teach at Michigan State?" The savvy candidates may expand on their answers, but nervous candidates may think that one or two words will provide all the information you want.
- **Ask open questions**: Open questions elicit expanded responses from the candidates and allow you to gauge their thought processes, values, reasons for decisions, and actual behaviors. "Would you explain the process you employ when developing curriculum?" or "How would you describe the nature of the courses that you taught at Wake Forest?"
- **Avoid leading questions:** Because leading questions suggest an answer, the candidate will feel compelled to agree with you. "You like working in teams, don't you?" or "Aren't statistics a challenge to teach?" Ask the questions in a more neutral way so that you get an honest answer: "How would you characterize your work in teams?" or "How do you feel about teaching statistics every spring semester?"
- **Use follow-up questions for complex subjects:** Rather than asking one long or complicated question, you can ask it in stages and follow up or probe as you go along. "What is your first step in curriculum development?" Later, "After the team has formulated a plan, what is your next step?"
- **Avoid hypothetical questions**. Creating scenarios to "test" your candidate yields no

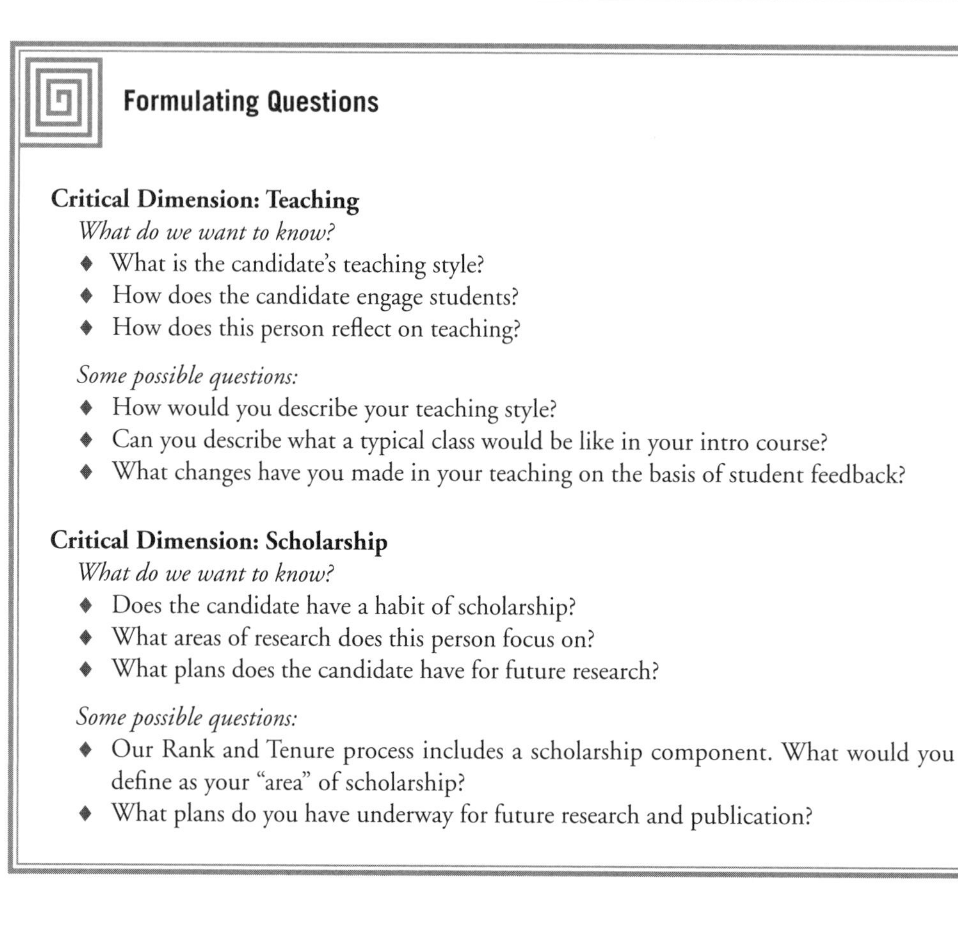

Formulating Questions

Critical Dimension: Teaching

What do we want to know?

- What is the candidate's teaching style?
- How does the candidate engage students?
- How does this person reflect on teaching?

Some possible questions:

- How would you describe your teaching style?
- Can you describe what a typical class would be like in your intro course?
- What changes have you made in your teaching on the basis of student feedback?

Critical Dimension: Scholarship

What do we want to know?

- Does the candidate have a habit of scholarship?
- What areas of research does this person focus on?
- What plans does the candidate have for future research?

Some possible questions:

- Our Rank and Tenure process includes a scholarship component. What would you define as your "area" of scholarship?
- What plans do you have underway for future research and publication?

valuable information about what this person would actually do on the job. Instead, hypothetical questions invite the "canned response." A familiar example of this occurs during campus interviews for Resident Advisor positions. The student applicants are frequently asked, "What would you do if you found your best friend violating the college alcohol policy in the residence halls?" The students always know to answer, "It doesn't matter how good a friend that person is. I would have to write them up for a disciplinary hearing." In actual practice, however, students tell us that an RA rarely writes up a friend for such a violation. This illustrates that hypothetical questions do not necessarily yield valid information about a candidate's actual behavior.

Recognizing Legal and Illegal Questions

It is simply amazing how few administrators and faculty members receive any guidance on developing effective interviewing questions. Many use illegal and inappropriate questions in employment interview situations, opening themselves and their institutions up to serious legal action. Most often, illegal questions are used in the context of casual conversations, such as dinner or a drive from the airport. See if you can detect which of the questions on page 41 would be considered illegal.

Are you surprised that *all* of the questions may potentially be illegal? The Equal Employment Opportunity and Affirmative Action (EEO/AA) guidelines for asking interview questions are rather restrictive and it is critical that the committee follows them. Here is an easy-to-remember rule:

Ask only questions that are bona fide occupational qualifications—BFOQs—questions directly related to a candidate's ability to do the job.

Limiting yourself to BFOQs will help you to stay out of legal trouble. There are a few other aspects of legal and illegal questions that you should know:

Which Questions Are Illegal?

- Ahmed is an unusual name. Where are you from originally?
- Will your wife need help in looking for employment in our community as well?
- Sometimes the college has open houses on Sundays. Would this interfere with your attending religious services?
- We have a great child care center on campus. Do you have any children?
- The students on this campus tend to be pretty conservative. How would you describe your political views?
- Would you like information about the quality of schools in the area?
- What is your native language?
- Have you ever been in the military?
- You don't look old enough to have a Ph.D.—how old are you?
- Have you ever been treated for mental illness?

1. EEO law relates to a group of protected classifications—this includes gender, race, nationality, age, disability, religion, and in some places sexual orientation. (Theoretically, you could be discriminated against because of eye color, since that is not a protected classification.) Stay away from questions that relate to these areas.
2. In some situations questions about the above areas may be legal. For example, if you work in a religious institution, a question about religion may be appropriate, *if it is a requirement for the applicant's ability to perform the job.* A religious institution that accepts no federal aid may require its employees to practice that particular religion. Employees may also be required to abide by some of the rules of that religion—for example, signing a pledge to abstain from alcohol.
3. If a candidate opens the door by asking about a particular area, then it is permissible for that topic to be discussed. For example, if a candidate says, "My husband is also an academic. Do you offer spousal relocation services?" it is appropriate to discuss this question.

The importance of understanding the use of BFOQs cannot be overestimated. The reputation of the institution can be jeopardized by the use of illegal and inappropriate questions at any time during the selection process.

Introducing Behavioral Event Interviewing

The purpose of the interview is to collect evidence of the candidate's ability to perform the job. The challenge is that the complete information is not readily accessible. Imagine the candidate as an iceberg. The information given on the resumé—the education and professional experiences—are above the water line. But to really gauge the depth of a candidate's abilities, you need to plumb below the water line, to explore areas such as motivators, values, and reasons for decisions. The questions you ask must illuminate these areas—the critical dimensions and personal qualities you have already determined are important for performing the job.

The richest information is drawn from stories that the candidates relate about their actual experience. This line of questioning is called "behavioral event" interviewing. In this approach, you ask the candidate for details about what they actually did, why they chose to do what they did, and the outcome of their behavior. Behavioral event questions are based on the assumption that past behavior predicts future behavior. We do this all the time—when we select students for scholarships or staff for special assignments, for example. In an interview situation, behavioral event questions zero in on the candidate's past behavior in the critical performance areas of the position. By asking the candidates for evidence of these critical dimensions from past situations in their lives, we can

Examples Worth Noting: Defining Legal/Illegal Questions

Example 1: What *CAN* you talk about? What *CAN'T* you talk about?

Le Von Wilson, J.D., Ed.D., from the College of Business, Western Carolina University, recently presented the following list of do's and don'ts for hiring interviews to Department Chairs and Deans at the Academic Chairs Conference:

What CAN you talk about?

- Work histories, references
- Ability to perform essential functions of the job
- Educational experience
- Interpersonal skills
- Potential starting date of employment
- Relationship with current or last employer
- Criminal convictions
- Career goals, objectives
- Salary, benefits, hours, working conditions

What CAN'T you talk about?

- Marital status
- Child care arrangements
- Health concerns (except to inquire if applicant can perform "essential functions" of the job)
- Arrest record (except in some states for security-sensitive positions)
- Religious affiliation (except for some church-affiliated institutions, certain positions)
- Childbearing or other family concerns

Example 2: Case Western Reserve University

Case Western Reserve University's website displays a very thorough chart on permissible inquiries to be used by its search committees, as shown on page 43.

theoretically predict their performance in similar situations at our own institutions.

Formulating Behavioral Event Questions

Formulating behavioral event questions is a straightforward process. Ask the candidate to describe actions taken in specific situations. Your question should stimulate a story from the candidate, which contains one or more examples. Elicit these three elements, or CARs:

Circumstances or context of the situation (What was going on at the time?)

Actions the candidate took (What did you actually do?)

Results or outcome of the actions (What happened? Why was that important?)

It will be necessary to ask probes or follow-up questions to determine the extent to which the candidate exhibited the behavior desired. The example on page 44 demonstrates the derivation of questions from a critical dimension and a personal attribute.

Subject	*Acceptable Inquiries*	*Unacceptable Inquiries*
Name	Whether the applicant has worked under another name.	Inquiries about the name that would seek to elicit information about the candidate's ancestry or descent. Inquiries about name change due to a court order, marriage, or otherwise.
Birthplace	See citizenship below.	Birthplace of applicant, spouse, parents, or other relatives.
Citizenship	Statement that employees must be eligible to work in the United States.	Any inquiries about citizenship or whether the applicant is or intends to becomes a U.S. citizen.
Residence Nationality	Place of residence Length of residence in this city.	Specific inquiries into foreign addresses that would indicate national origin, nationality of applicant. Whether applicant owns or rents home.
Age	Can inquire if applicant meets minimum age requirements, or state that proof may be required upon hiring.	Cannot require that applicant state age or date of birth. Cannot require that applicant submit proof of age before hiring. Any questions that may tend to identify applicants over 40 years of age.
Sex	Inquiry or restriction of employment is permissible only when a BFOQ exists.	Any inquiry that would indicate sex of applicant. Applicant's sex cannot be used as a factor for determining whether an applicant will be "satisfied" in a particular job.
Marital and family status, sexual identity	Whether applicant can meet specific work schedules.	Marital status or number of dependents. Names, ages, or addresses of spouse, children, or relatives. Questions about sexual identity, orientation, or preference.
Race, color, physical	Voluntary submission of AA/EEO information is made directly to the Office of Equal Employment and Diversity.	Inquiry as to applicant's race, color of skin, eyes, or hair or other questions directly or indirectly indicating race or color. Applicant's height or weight when it is not relevant to the job.
Disability	Can ask an applicant questions about his or her ability to perform job-related functions.	General inquiries ("Are you disabled?") that would tend to reveal disability or health conditions that do not relate to fitness to perform the job.
Education	Applicant's academic, vocational attainment.	Date last attended high school (reflects age).
Pregnancy	No acceptable inquiry.	Any question concerning pregnancy or birth control.
Arrests and convictions	Asking about conviction of a crime related to job qualification.	Asking about arrests.
Religion	No acceptable inquiry.	Any question requesting the applicant's religious affiliation, church, parish, pastor, or religious holidays observed.
Military Experience	If needed for employment history, you may ask about applicant's military experience in the U.S. Armed Forces.	Any question into applicant's general military experience. Any question into type of discharge.
Organizations	Any question into applicant's membership in organizations which the applicant considers relevant to his/her ability to perform the job.	Asking what organizations, clubs, and societies the applicant belongs to that are not relevant to his/her ability to perform the job (political, social, religious, etc.)

Developing a Behavioral Event Question

Critical Dimension: Consensus building and collegial teamwork; potential to assume department leadership in two to three years.

Points raised by the Search Committee: No prior departmental level leadership mentioned on the resumé; outstanding academic leadership but no evidence of collaborative teaching, presentations, or publications; no details given on academic or administrative committee involvement; three community leadership roles of three to five years duration.

Behavioral Question: From time to time, all of us encounter colleagues who disagree with us. We'd like you to think of a time when you were a leader or team member and your recommendations for action were challenged by a colleague. Perhaps you were working with others in your department or on a committee. We'd like to hear about a situation like that. What were the circumstances at the time? What specific actions or steps did you take to handle the situation? With whom did you interact ? Finish by telling us how the situation turned out.

Additional Examples of Behavioral Event Questions

- Tell me about a successful collaborative project you worked on in the past year. With whom did you work? What was your role? How did it turn out?
- How did you market your new program to the intended participants? Who did you have to work with to pull it off? What happened? What, if anything, would you do differently the next time? Why?
- What was the most challenging counseling situation you had last year? How did you approach it? What steps did you take to address it? What was the outcome?
- We'd like you to think of an example where you were responsible for organizing and coordinating a major initiative in your department. How did you approach the task? Walk me through the steps. How did you evaluate its effectiveness? How did the initiative work out?

The committee should include some behavioral event questions in the interview. You will be amazed at the depth of insight you gain about the candidates from what they reveal to you. This is the substance that truly defines their fit for the position and the institution.

Training Other Campus Constituencies for Interviewing

In addition to the search committee, your candidates will meet with other members of the campus community—faculty, staff, administrators, and students. You need to be sure these constituencies understand their role in the interview process. They must receive some direction to be sure that they do not violate any EEO/AA guidelines.

We have had positive experiences from inviting campus constituents to participate in a short, general meeting on interviewing protocol, supplemented by a brief handout on conducting an interview. The handout details the intention of the meeting with the candidate, suggests a format, gives guidelines and suggestions about questions, and specifies illegal questions and topics.

See page 45 for an example of a memo e-mailed to a constituent group.

You should also provide these constituencies with a simple feedback form designed to give you consistent feedback for evaluating the candidates. It's wise to review the form and how to complete it during the interview training session. One form for students to use in evaluating a faculty candidate is shown on page 46.

Dear Members of the Student Government Executive Committee,

On behalf of the Search Committee for the Dean of Student Affairs, I want to thank you for scheduling a 45-minute meeting with each of the three final candidates in the next two weeks. The selection of a new Dean is a major undertaking. The people we recommend to the President and the person she selects will influence the course of our college for many years to come. Your role in the decision is significant. Your input on each candidate from the perspective of your members and the goals of the student government will be factored into our recommendation to the President. We appreciate that you are taking this role seriously.

The following arrangements have been made for your meetings:

Place: Gleason 218
Time: 2:00–2:45 p.m.
Dates: Tuesday 4/15, Friday, 4/18, and Friday 4/25
Expectations: We ask that you:

- start and complete your meeting on time
- designate a member present to escort the candidate to the next interview (itineraries attached)
- provide feedback using the enclosed form
- appoint a member to collect and deliver the feedback forms to Gil Shores in his office in Basil Hall 319
- ask position-focused questions and interact with each candidate in a manner that represents the College in a positive light
- carefully review the packet of information which will be provided on each candidate three days before the campus interview
- maintain confidentiality in all aspects of the search.

To support your contribution to the Dean search, we invite you to participate in a one-hour interviewing training program designed specifically for this search process. The training will be held on 4/8 in Ward Hall 110 from 1:00–2:00 p.m. Developed and delivered by Karen Gauger of the Human Resources Department and Mary Witherspoon of the Career Services Office, it covers how to ask good questions, what are legal and illegal questions, how to actively listen to the candidate's responses, and what are the rules of confidentiality. Time is allowed at the end for you to practice formulating and asking a question in a simulated interview.

Asking the right interview questions is a skill that, once mastered, will serve you well throughout your life, both as a job candidate and as a supervisor of others. Won't you join other student representatives, selected faculty and staff, and the search committee in this program to improve our interviewing skills? Reserve your place by replying to this email.

Thank you again for your participation and anticipated contributions.

Dr. Sanjeev Sethapathy
Chair—Dean's Search Committee

Enc.: itineraries, feedback forms

Student's name: ____________________

Name of Candidate: ____________________

Please fill out the evaluation form and make any additional comments below.

History Department Faculty Evaluation

Dimensions	Exceptional	Above Average	Good	Below Average	Unable to Judge
1. Teaching Demonstration					
2. Academic Advising					
3. Career Counseling					
4. History Club Advisor					

Other comments:

Thank you for your participation in this interview process! Please return this form to David Greer in Anderson 270 by 5:00 p.m. today.

Checklist for Preparing to Interview

- ❒ Formulated the structure of the interview
- ❒ Conducted interview training for the committee members as a group
- ❒ Planned the agenda
- ❒ Reviewed the use of legal and illegal questions
- ❒ Planned and formulated questions for the interview
- ❒ Assessed that the balance of questions are open-ended and some are behavioral
- ❒ Reviewed questions for their focus on the critical dimensions and for legality
- ❒ Conducted training for other constituents involved in the interview process
- ❒ Developed feedback form for other constituencies

References

Faculty Search Committee Guidelines, Case Western Reserve University, Office of Equal Opportunity and Diversity. Retrieved 02/24/05 from www.case.edu/finadmin/humres/eod/facultysearchguide.pdf

Wilson, L. E. (2004). *Academic administrators and the law: Avoiding lawsuits in higher education.* Paper presented to the Academic Chairs Conference, Orlando, FL.

CHAPTER 6

Preliminary Screening Interviews

In this chapter, you will

- Address logistical issues of phone screens
- Plan for conducting phone or teleconference screens
- Evaluate and rank candidates after the phone screen
- Consider the variables of using professional conferences to screen candidates

Getting Started

NOW THAT YOU'VE CHOSEN the high-potential candidates, you're ready to plan the phone interview process. Even after carefully screening and ranking the resumés, you may still have a number of candidates to assess. It's tempting to "get on with it" and call in the candidates you want to interview as soon as possible. Compelling as it is, we encourage you to curb your impulse and carefully plan the next screening step, which is typically a phone screen.

The purpose of a phone screen is to eliminate unqualified or undesirable candidates and to identify the top candidates you want to pursue. Phone screens are an efficient and effective method for reducing your candidate pool to those whose qualifications most closely match your position description and whose personal attributes fit your culture. Because phone screens are relatively short in duration, the committee can move through this step rather quickly.

Planning for the Phone Screen

Phone screens are usually about thirty minutes long. After the initial greeting, you will ask several questions. Use the first few questions to verify the information on the candidate's resumé. Follow these with open-ended questions that probe into areas of interest or concern to you. When you develop specifically targeted questions for each candidate, you'll be amazed at the quality of the information this process reveals. This may also be the time when you feel out the candidate's expectations regarding compensation by either stating the salary range for the position or by inquiring about the range that the candidate is looking for. The components of a typical phone screen are displayed on page 48.

Targeting Questions for Each Candidate

The value of the interview process is directly related to the quality of the questions you ask. You have already developed a general interview agenda (Chapter 5). To develop powerful questions that advance your agenda, ask each member to come to the search committee meeting armed with all the resumés and the screening forms they completed for each candidate in the pool. Go through the screening forms candidate by candidate and identify areas of concern, incomplete information, and need for greater detail. The contrast of members' perspectives and their mix of perceptions are the source of your questions. Because each candidate offers different strengths and experiences, the specific questions will differ for each.

It's enlightening to hear how one member's red flag is another's green light. To illustrate, in a recent search one committee member advocated for eliminating a

Structure of a Thirty-Minute Phone Screen

Time	*Purpose of the Question*	*Sampling of Questions*
5 min	Verifying information	1. Walk me through the last 10 years. 2. Why did you make that move? 3. In what year did you complete that?
15 min	Determining fit, qualifications, and interest	1. Tell me about yourself. 2. What do you know about us? 3. What attracted you to this position? 4. Tell us about a time when . . .
3–5 min	Answering questions from the candidate	What questions do you have for us?
3–5 min	Next steps	We will be interviewing a few more candidates in the next 10 days. You will hear from us by the 15th of the month about our decision.

candidate because he had so many two- to three-year employment entries over the previous ten years. Another committee member noted that the candidate had held two to three *concurrent* positions over several years that had allowed him to gain considerable experience in the environments desired for their position. The questions they developed for this candidate were directed at his reasons for wanting their position and his satisfaction with a single-focus career choice.

Setting the Appointment

To set up the phone interview appointment, the candidate can be called or e-mailed by a committee member or an administrative assistant. Make sure that the number at which you reached the candidate is the number to be called for the phone interview. If not, it is crucial that the correct number be noted on the copies of the resumé distributed to all the committee members. Things happen; more than one member needs to know where to call the candidate if the lead interviewer is unexpectedly unable to place the call.

We have found that the scheduling process can be expedited by asking committee members to designate certain times of the week for search committee business so that candidates can be quickly plugged into those time slots. When members commit to being available at those times, the interview schedule can be readily concluded. If you plan to conduct multiple phone screens on the same day, allow ample time between interviews so that one unexpected event does not disrupt the remaining interviews. The time between interviews allows the committee members present to note their impressions of the candidate and discuss their reactions while they are fresh.

Designating the Interviewers

Some committees select designated members to conduct the interviews. Others expect each member to assume some role in the interviews. Other committees expect all the members to interview every candidate. The interpersonal dynamic of the candidate is a key factor in the selection process, but it is challenging to describe to others who were not present. We recommend that every member be present for at least one interview session, whether or not they choose to ask any questions. With the candidate's prior knowledge, the interview can be taped for absent members to listen to and reference later, if necessary.

Resolving Logistical Considerations

Phone screens typically last about thirty minutes. They can be conducted from a single source where committee members talk to the candidate in a conference call, or the interview can be conducted from individual members' offices by calling them on a conference line. With careful planning, both strategies are effective. It's critical that cell phones and pagers be turned off, and that potential distractions and interruptions be anticipated and minimized.

Videoconference Interviews
Arranging a videoconference interview is another strategy that's growing in popularity, especially when qualifications for the position include presentation skills or personal presence. Most academic institutions as well as major metropolitan areas typically have videoconferencing capabilities that you can contract with. A videoconference interview was chosen by a small liberal arts college for a faculty candidate who lived a continent away. The search committee used the videoconference after the phone screen as an intermediate step to determine whether they would spend 30 percent of their limited budget on a $1500 airline ticket to bring the candidate to campus.

Using videoconferencing presents a few interesting challenges. If you decide to use it, here are some issues to keep in mind:

- Ask the candidates if they are aware of resources convenient to their location. If they are currently employed in a university, they may have access to videoconference capabilities in the communications, career, or media departments. Typically you would make the arrangements for scheduling and paying for the videoconference.
- Double check the time difference between your location and the candidate's location to be sure you call at the correct time.
- Schedule a trial run to acclimate to the equipment. There is often a delay between when you speak and when the sound is heard by the candidate (and you), and the ensuing "echo" can be disconcerting and awkward until you get used to it.
- Decide where members should sit for optimum communication and personal presentation.
- Notice the surroundings—what impression does the visual environment communicate to the candidate?
- Orchestrate the interview well—videoconference time is expensive.
- Agree on a back-up plan. If the videoconference connection fails, what will you do?

Videotaped Interviews
What can you do if calling the candidate is problematic? For example, what if the candidate is deaf or hard of hearing, or lives in Asia where there is a significant time difference from the Unites States? Some institutions have successfully used videotaped interviews. In a videotaped interview, the candidate answers your prepared questions on tape, and then sends you the tape. The questions should be fairly consistent with the questions you pose to the other candidates by phone.

Organizing Your Materials
Everyone should have a copy of the agenda as well as the candidate's resumé and cover letter. It helps to prepare the questions in print form and distribute them to members prior to the interview. This allows the members engaged in the interview to rehearse the questions assigned to them and to anticipate their follow-up questions. Using a standardized agenda that includes all the questions allows the interviewers to capture the candidate's responses in a consistent manner and to easily compare notes after the interview. The interview room should have a visible clock so that the lead interviewer can keep the interview on schedule. It also helps to supply additional pencils and pens, clean paper, tissues, and perhaps a tape recorder or laptop, if electronic recording of the interview is desired and permitted.

Conducting the Phone Screen Interview

For efficiency and professional presentation, one member should be designated as the lead interviewer. In this capacity, the lead member greets the candidate, explains the logistics, introduces the other members present, orchestrates the flow, and assures that the agenda of the interview is accomplished. Some search committees have assigned critical dimensions to specific members who are responsible for asking the questions related to that area. For example, one member may focus on leadership and management while another concentrates on interpersonal dimensions and communication. Members need to know what questions they and the other members will ask and agree prior to the interview whether others can jump in with unplanned or follow-up questions. If this contingency is not addressed prior to the interviews, well-meaning probes can derail the interview. A sample agenda for a phone screen appears at the end of this chapter on page 54.

During the interview, each member actively listens to the responses of the candidate. Your role is to seek and make note of evidence that substantiates the candidate's match with your needs. Pay attention to your feelings about the candidate from the nonverbal cues and interpersonal dynamics. For example, does the candidate answer the questions efficiently and in a straightforward manner? Is the candidate argumentative? Does the candidate sound likeable and pleasant? Reveal a sense of humor? Compassion? Sensitivity to issues of diversity?

In the last segment of the phone screen, you invite the candidate to ask questions. By inviting the candidates to ask questions, you can pay attention to the focus and concerns their questions reveal. Is the candidate concerned about politics, the resources available, salary issues, support for scholarly research, the time frame for hiring, the nature of the student body, governance? Just as in your questions to the candidate, behind every question is a need or concern. What are the issues important to this candidate? Make note of them—they probably hold the key to solidifying an offer to the candidate of choice.

At the conclusion of the phone interview, give the candidate some indication of your time frame for moving the search to the next step and a commitment to communicate your decision in a timely manner. In the midst of interviewing a number of candidates and balancing your other obligations, two to three weeks fly by; to the candidate, that's an eternity. Many institutions lose the respect of candidates by not communicating with them and by disregarding their needs in the process. This mistake could haunt you in the future. By representing your institution as one that appreciates the investment made by the candidate, you elevate its reputation in the world of current and future candidates. So have a good understanding of your search process time line and be prepared to speak to that at the conclusion of the phone screen.

Rating and Ranking the Screened Candidates

Immediately following the phone screen, the committee members who are present should discuss the candidate. Air concerns. Cite evidence of where the candidate meets, exceeds, or falls short of your desired qualifications and personal attributes. Go back to your profile; did the phone interview change your initial impressions? How does this candidate now compare to the other candidates?

The specific ranking form that you use for candidates interviewed during a phone screen should be directly related to the critical dimensions the committee wishes to address. An example of a phone screen feedback form is on page 55 at the end of this chapter.

Using the critical dimensions from the screening form, indicate whether you will recommend that the search committee pursue or eliminate this candidate, or postpone a decision until all the phone interviews are complete.

When all the candidates have been interviewed by phone, convene the full committee to review and prioritize the candidates. Because all members may not have participated in each of the interviews, this meeting serves to cull outstanding candidates and eliminate others. It is likely that a few outstanding candidates will rise to the top of the pile, a number will fall out of consideration, and others will be of moderate interest and worth keeping in the pool. Move the outstanding candidates to the next level—the on-campus interview. Ideally, this group will include at least two and no more than seven candidates. The candidates whom you do not want to pursue should be notified immediately. However, be careful about eliminating the candidates in whom you still have moderate interest. Depending on the outcome of the on-site interviews, you may want to keep them active. To do this, it's respectful to communicate to these candidates that the process may take longer than anticipated.

Eliminating Candidates

There are a number of reasons for disqualifying and eliminating candidates at this stage of the process. A list of reasons is shown on page 51. What other reasons have you encountered?

At the point you decide to eliminate a candidate, communicate your decision quickly by letter. Although e-mails are gaining popularity as a primary means of communication, we suggest that you send candidates a well-written, personalized letter. Candidates genuinely appreciate an indication of the reason they were eliminated from the pool. A rejection letter appears on page 51.

Does your institution expect a candidate log that documents the outcome of each candidate in the process? Many public institutions do, and the colleges and universities concerned about advancing diversity

Reasons for Disqualifying Candidates

- Research emphasis is not in the preferred area or is irrelevant or tangential to the position.
- Communication skills did not meet expectations.
- The candidate has insufficient publications.
- Degree requirements are not complete.
- The candidate's background is not a match for the position.
- The candidate withdrew from consideration.
- The candidate has insufficient experience in a key area.
- The candidate exhibited undesirable or unacceptable behavior or comments.

are likely to expect this accountability from the search committee. The search committee chair is responsible for seeing that this log is completed as each candidate moves through the process (see Chapter 1), so now is the time to update it.

Interviewing at Professional Conferences

In addition to phone and videoconferences, some initial screening for academic positions may take place at professional academic conferences. These may be intentional or coincidental. For example, our colleagues in the English Department make a special recruiting trip to the Modern Languages Association (MLA) Convention each December specifically to meet prospective candidates. On the other hand, a professor who happened to be presenting a paper at the Association for Education in Journalism and Mass Communication (AEJMC) spent some time in the Placement Center speaking with candidates interested in a position open in the Communication/Journalism Department. Regardless of the reason for your interviewing at conferences, they can be valuable early contacts with

Sample Rejection Letter

Dear Professor Clark:

The Search Committee would like to thank you for your interest in the position of Dean of the College of Engineering. We were pleased to have the opportunity to speak with you during our phone screen and to review your qualifications.

While your background and qualifications are strong, there are other candidates with more experience in the administrative and assessment areas. We feel these candidates more closely align with our needs at the present time.

Thank you for allowing us to consider you for this position. We wish you continued success in your career pursuits.

Sincerely,

Shirley Wright
Search Committee Chair

potential candidates for your current or prospective positions.

While interviewing candidates at professional conferences is a viable alternative to phone screening, these interviews do necessitate some adjustments to the logistics presented above. Any member of a search committee attending a professional conference should use the standard agenda from the committee to ensure that the questions asked of conference candidates are consistent with the questions asked of all applicants. Some candidates may send their dossiers ahead of time, so you can customize the agenda for particular individuals; other candidates may just "show up" at the conference placement center for an impromptu interview. In either case, it's important to have a plan to follow.

It is also helpful for the search committee representative to have some literature to provide interested candidates. In a recent faculty search, we sent one of our representatives to a conference with copies of the position description, college view books from the Admissions office, department brochures and publications, and copies of the campus newspaper. This enabled our representative to personalize the process a little more and gave the applicants more information about the school and the program to which they were applying. Out of five candidates who met with our representative, two ended up with on-campus interviews and one landed the position.

In addition to pre-planning the agenda of placement center interviews, you will probably also need to address some interesting logistical challenges at the conference. Mark and Lorraine Serva of the University of Delaware made several recommendations for interviewing at professional conferences based on their research on tenure-track job interviews for management information system positions.

Tips for Interviewing at Conferences

- Designated interviewing areas at conferences tend to be noisy and distracting for both the interviewer and candidate. Interviewers should attempt to find a setting more conducive to effective interviewing, such as seating in low-traffic areas of the hotel.
- Conference interviewers may wish to book rooms on the hotel's concierge floor, since the concierge areas are often underutilized during the day and can offer a quiet alternative.
- Interviewers should also consider area restaurants, parks, and even shopping malls, all less formal settings that can be a good opportunity for relaxed conversation, especially during off-peak hours.
- While hotel rooms are typically quiet and more conducive to open dialogue, interviewing in hotel rooms can increase the possibility of litigation, especially when interviewing a candidate of the opposite sex. If universities plan to use hotel rooms for interviews, they should be willing to send multiple interviewers; ideally one interviewer should be a woman.
- Regardless of the setting, interviewers need to be aware of the use of inappropriate questions in selection interviews. Even when using an informal setting such as a restaurant or a hotel lobby, interviewers' questions must remain within the constraints of the law.

Dealing with Internal Candidates

In faculty and administrative searches, it is not unusual to have internal candidates in the pool. An adjunct or temporary faculty member may apply for a tenure-track opening, a faculty member may want to move to an administrative post, or an entry-level administrator may desire a promotion. Regardless of the position and the person's connection with your school, internal candidates should be treated in the same manner as all other candidates. This means that you review, select, interview, present, or eliminate them using the same process and criteria as all the other applicants. "Courtesy interviews" are unfair to the applicant and waste valuable time of the search committee.

In the case of a phone screen, an internal candidate—or one who lives locally—may suggest that he or she just come in for a face-to-face meeting with the search committee. Resist following this suggestion. Even if the candidate is only fifty feet from your office, follow the same protocol for all candidates and insist on a phone screen. This protects the integrity of the process and minimizes the likelihood that the propriety or legality of the search practices will be questioned after an offer is made.

Checklist for Preliminary Screening Interview

- ❐ Planned the agenda for phone screens
- ❐ Convened committee members to identify, draft, and delegate questions for each candidate
- ❐ Scheduled interviews
- ❐ Assigned lead interviewer and questioner roles
- ❐ Prepared logistics for each interview
- ❐ Anticipated contingencies and minimized disruptions
- ❐ Reviewed and adapted recordkeeping materials
- ❐ Stocked the interview room, checked the phone equipment, and tested the conference call capability
- ❐ Eliminated and notified unqualified candidates
- ❐ Tracked outcomes of phone screens for all candidates

Potential Pitfalls

- **Failure to plan adequately for phone screens.** While a casual conversation might give you a good idea about the personality of the individual candidate, your time is wasted if you don't zero in on key areas of concern to the committee.
- **Failure to be sensitive to diversity.** Have you made every reasonable attempt to screen for inclusion rather than exclusion? Have you been careful not to eliminate someone merely on the basis of an alternative career path?
- **Lack of attractive prospects after phone screens.** If none of the candidates seem appropriate for the position after you have finished your phone interviews, the committee needs to return to the person who charged the committee and discuss reopening the search. At this point, the committee may also need to go back to its early stages to see if any flaws in the process might be responsible for the lack of response from attractive candidates.

Reference

Serva, M. A., & Serva, L. C. (2001) So, where are you from originally? Using ineffective and inappropriate questions in MIS tenure-track job interviews. *Journal of Information Systems Education, 12* (1), 15–22.

Sample Agenda for Phone Screen

Candidate: Jean Poole   Date: 7/14

Interview conducted by: Harold and Peg

1. Harold: Welcome, introductions, overview of interview
   a. Provide brief outline of the process.
   b. Note that Peg and Harold will be alternating questions.
2. Harold: Verify information
   a. Walk us through career progression; begin with your education and highlight the experiences you believe are relevant for this position.
   b. Tell us about your Toronto University experience.
3. Peg: Fit
   a. What do you know about our institution?
   b. Tell us about your experience in a small, independent college like ours.
   c. What are you looking for in your next position?
4. Harold: Program director role
   a. As the new education director, what initial steps would you take to establish your leadership?
   b. Describe the relationship that you would want to establish with the president and the provost.
   c. In prior jobs, what did you do to foster positive working relationships with your new staff and your supervisor?
5. Peg: Leadership, consensus
   a. As a director, how did you assure the productivity and satisfaction of your direct reports and staff? Can you give us an example?
   b. Can you give us an example of a recent leadership challenge you have had to face in the workplace?
6. Harold: NCATE accreditation
   a. What is your experience in designing assessment programs to satisfy NCATE accreditation?
   b. Can you tell us about a particular instance when your assessment led you to introduce a new program or process?
7. Peg: What questions do you have for us?
   a. Note each question asked.
   b. Note substance of response to the candidate—is there follow-up needed?
8. Harold: Next steps and close
   a. Timeline
   b. Thank the candidate

Phone Screen Feedback Form

Name of Applicant: Jean Poole

Name of Committee Member: ______________________________

Listed below are the topics we discussed in Dr. Poole's phone screen. Please note your comments for each topic and your overall evaluation.

1. Fit for position:
   a. What she knows
   b. Experience in small college
   c. What she's looking for
2. Program Director Role
   a. Initial steps
   b. Establishing and sustaining relationships with president/provost
   c. Establishing and sustaining relationships with staff/supervisor
3. Leadership, consensus
   a. Evidence of ensuring productivity and satisfaction of staff
   b. Leadership qualities evidenced by challenge situation
4. NCATE experience
   a. Assessment programs
   b. Outcomes
5. Her questions
6. Follow-up commitments

Comments: __________

____

____

____

____

____

____

______ campus interview ______ hold ______ eliminate

Reasons for eliminating candidate:

CHAPTER 7

The Campus Interviews

In this chapter, you will

- Determine the logistics and an itinerary for campus interviews
- Develop an agenda of topics for the search committee meeting
- Prepare other campus constituencies
- Create and maintain dialogue with your candidate
- Ensure that the candidate is welcomed and made comfortable
- Conduct the interview in a timely and professional way
- Troubleshoot the unexpected

Getting Started

YOU'RE READY TO INVITE the final candidates to campus and meet them face-to-face. Your first step should be deciding what you can reasonably handle in terms of time and frequency of these campus visits. The pace can be hectic, the time demands are significant, and, in the context of an academic semester, the pressure can be enormous. Some search committees elect to space out their campus interviews, doing one or two per week. One of our searches took place each Tuesday and Thursday for two weeks to include four finalists—they were the only days of the week when we had the time to meet with the candidates. Another search we were involved in had four finalists in four days—a grueling pace, but the comparisons among candidates were obvious and the process was over in a relatively short time.

Preparing for the On-campus Interview

Once you decide when you can meet with the candidates, you need to contact them to secure their availability. Be sure that you provide candidates with flexibility to work around their schedules as well as yours.

After scheduling the on-campus interview, be sure to send each finalist a written confirmation and a packet of information about your institution and the local area. This should include additional information that would not be found easily on the web site, such as:

- A college catalogue
- A college view book or other recruiting documents from Admissions
- A copy of the strategic plan, if available
- College publications, such as campus newspaper, campus newsletter, alumni magazine, literary magazine
- Area information from the Chamber of Commerce and visitor's center for those who live outside the area
- A detailed agenda for the visit
- Any background information needed in preparation for meetings with different constituencies
- An organizational chart of the college that also shows where the position they are interviewing for fits in
- A detailed description of any presentation they will be required to deliver during the interview day

Determining the Itinerary

There are some aspects of the campus visit that are "givens" for each candidate. These include meetings with the search committee, with the person who charged the committee, and with Human Resources, as well as a tour of the campus.

Beyond these obvious choices, the committee has a great deal of discretion for scheduling the candidates' itinerary. The first consideration should be the constituencies interested in the candidate. These may include students, staff reports, administrators, and other faculty who will be working in close contact with the new hire. When recruiting diversity candidates, you might include representatives from minority or ethnic groups on campus or from the community, perhaps even from institutions in close proximity. If there are many people who wish to or need to meet the candidates on this list, you may consider group interviews. For example, candidates for a Dean's position might meet with the Registrar, Director of Financial Aid, and Director of Career Services in a group interview.

You may also wish to see your candidate "in action," especially a candidate for a faculty position. Many academic departments ask the candidates to present a paper, as if they were at a professional conference. The presentation may be to department faculty, faculty and students, or open to the campus community. Other departments ask the candidates to teach a class—we have found this to be one of the most revealing sessions in evaluating faculty candidates. (One candidate who came across very strong in his faculty and administrative meetings literally put some students to sleep during his class!) Whatever you choose, give your candidates enough time to prepare for the presentation. Also make sure presentation resources are available and technical support is provided for multimedia talks.

Finally, in scheduling your campus itinerary, you need to allow enough time to accomplish all the meetings planned, to get to and from each event, and to give your candidates a little "down time." This is especially considerate of the candidate who visits for an entire day—or perhaps two days in the case of a high-level administrator. Also, the committee needs to decide who will escort the candidates to and from each event—it could be one person, but generally committee members like to divide up the tasks. The conversations between appointments may be excellent opportunities to get to know the candidates on a more personal and informal basis.

We present a sample itinerary for a faculty candidate in Psychology on page 59.

Determining the Agenda for the Search Committee Meeting with the Candidate

A key element of the campus visit will be the candidate's meeting with the search committee. You need to allow an hour and a half to two hours for this important time. This is when the search committee follows up on the critical dimensions that were approached in the phone screen. The following are some tips for planning the search committee meeting:

- Plan an agenda for the meeting using the critical dimensions you have identified, with questions about the most important dimensions being asked first (Chapter 6).
- Ask questions within a particular topic area before moving on to the next. The better organized you are, the easier it will be for the candidate to answer fully and give you the information you need to make the decision.
- Assign specific individuals to cover each of the key topic areas. The interview yields the most productive results when the candidate feels confident and relaxed. Multiple committee members firing questions at the same time will increase the tension and make it harder for you to discern whether the answer fits the information you are seeking.
- Be sure to allow fifteen to twenty minutes of the meeting time for the candidates to ask their own questions. Try to answer to the best of your ability, but if you don't know the answer to a question, promise to find out and get back to them. Also remember that you are gaining valuable insights about the candidates by the nature of the questions they ask. (For example, would you want to hire a faculty candidate whose first question is, "What is the salary for this position?")

The search committee agenda for the Psychology candidate appears on page 59.

Once you agree on the agenda, you still need to apportion your time to be sure you cover each of the topic areas. Figure 1 (p. 60) shows the approximate time division recommended for a one-hour search committee meeting with a candidate. Planning for more time will give you some flexibility, but the proportions should remain the same.

Campus Itinerary for Dr. Amanda B. Reckonwith, Dept. of Psychology

Monday, April 3:

4 p.m.: Arrive at airport (picked up by Dr. Gonzales)

6 p.m.: Dinner at hotel restaurant with Search Committee

Tuesday, April 4:

8 a.m.: Breakfast at hotel with Dr. Backus, Chair, Psych. Dept.

9 a.m.: Arrive on campus and campus tour (Dr. Backus will bring candidate to Admissions office for student tour)

10 a.m.: Meet with Provost (escort by Dr. Phillips)
- Admin. Bldg. 106

10:30 a.m.: Meet with Human Resources (escort by Dr. Sims)
- Admin. Bldg. 211

11 a.m.: Teach a class in cognitive psych. (escorted by Dr. Sims)
- Fellows Hall Room 112

12 noon: Lunch with Psych Club students (escort by Jean Baker)
- Faculty Dining Room, Commons Bldg.

1 p.m.: Meet with Search Committee
- Library Room 319

3 p.m.: Meet with director of psych lab (escort by Dr. Tang)
- Psych Lab, Fellows Hall 200

3:30 p.m.: Conclusion with Dept. Chair (Fellows Hall 231)

4 p.m.: Drive to airport (Dr. Horton)

Search Committee Agenda: Dr. Reckonwith

Tuesday, April 4
1:00 p.m.
Library—Room 319

- Introduction and overview of interview: Dr. Backus
- Interest in the position and College: Dr. Backus
- Teaching: Dr. Tang
- Work in lab: Dr. Tang
- Scholarship and professional activities: Dr. Sims
- Service: Dr. Gonzales
- Advising experience: Dr. Gonzales
- Collegiality, willingness to work with other faculty, team teach: Dr. Tang (if time)
- Candidate's questions: Dr. Backus
- Conclusion/next steps: Dr. Backus

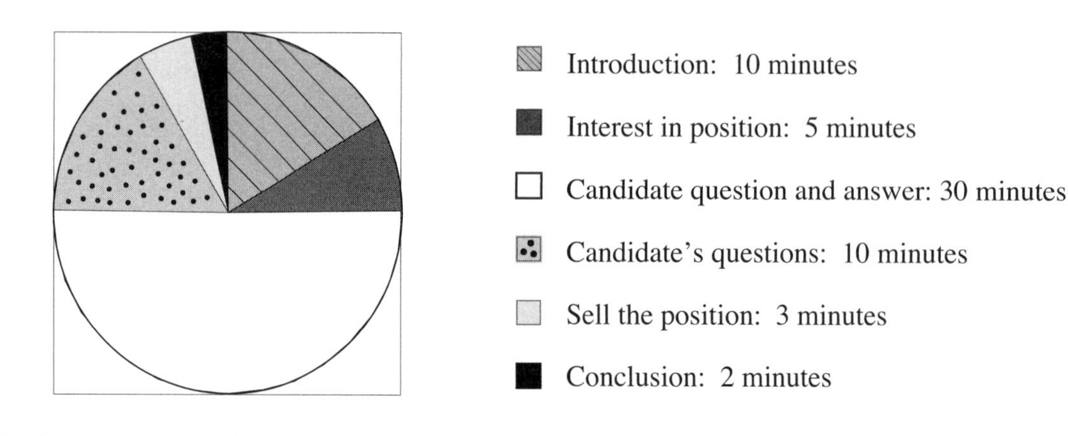

Figure 7.1 Search committee interview time division allotment.

Meetings with Other Constituencies
In addition to meeting with the search committee, your candidate will also have interviews with various constituent groups. Logistics for constituent meetings with candidates should be handled through the search committee to ensure that the meetings occur and are held in an appropriate venue. However, search committee members should not be present. These meetings allow the candidate to ask questions and explore cultural and social considerations outside the scope of the search committee. Ask each constituent present to complete a simple feedback form like the one in chapter 5 (p. 46) commenting on the affect, interaction, and overall impression made by the candidate. A space on the form can be reserved for concerns, specific comments, and issues raised by the candidate. Identify one person from the meeting to collect and ensure the delivery of the feedback forms to a designated member of the committee.

The Actual On-Campus Interview

Now that you have planned your campus interviews carefully, you should be free to focus on your candidates and determine their fit for your position. Your task at this stage is to follow the plan, observe, listen, dialogue, and take very good notes.

Creating and Maintaining Dialogue
It is important for the search committee to designate one key person as the contact individual for each of the candidates. This may be the chair or a different contact person for each finalist. The contact person's responsibilities include:

- Contacting the candidate the day before the scheduled arrival to confirm travel and schedule information
- Providing the candidate with office phone, home phone, and cell phone numbers to contact in case of emergency
- Providing the candidate one other contact number in case he or she is unable to reach the primary contact person—for example, the department administrative assistant's number
- Confirming with the search committee and other campus constituencies that the scheduled meetings are on their calendars
- Maintaining contact with the candidate through arrival, the campus visit, and departure, to resolve any issues that may arise
- Following up after the interview to ensure that the candidate arrived home safely and to address any further questions

Ensuring the Candidate is Welcomed and Made Comfortable
All of the research shows that you will be more successful in your interviews if you create a climate of trust for the candidates, while avoiding anything that may cause your guests undue stress. To this end, keep the following tips in mind:

- Confirm with your candidates who will be meeting them and how to recognize that person. Then be sure the greeter is there on time to welcome them.
- Confirm hotel reservations for each candidate and be sure that the school, not the candidate, is charged. You don't want the candidate to deal with a request to pay the bill or provide a credit card at check-in. It is nice to provide a welcome basket in the hotel room as well as an updated itinerary for the interview and any additional information about the campus—for example, the most recent issue of the campus newspaper.
- For the interviews, choose private and comfortable rooms that afford the candidates the best opportunity to sell their qualities. These may not necessarily be the rooms most convenient for you. For example, even though it means a walk across the campus (sometimes in inclement weather), one department chair always reserves a particular room in the library for interviews, because it is isolated and provides a comfortable atmosphere for the search committee session with candidates.

Conducting the Interview in a Timely and Professional Way

Brendan's Story

I was just finishing my Ph.D. and was excited to be invited to an on-campus interview at a major East Coast university several hundred miles from my home. I did thorough research on the school and the program, flew in the night before to get a good night's sleep, and arrived promptly at 10 a.m. as requested. Imagine my surprise when I heard the search committee was not ready for me! It turned out that the committee had scheduled more than one interview that day and they were terribly behind schedule. After spending several hours with the department secretary and visiting a class in the program, I got in to meet the Search Committee for barely 30 minutes *before I had to leave for the airport to catch my flight home. After this interviewing nightmare, I was even more surprised when the department chair offered me the position! Of course, even a new Ph.D. in lean economic times knew better than to accept a position with a department that showed so little regard for its candidates.*

Don't forget that while you are evaluating the candidates for your position, they are, at the same time, evaluating you. How the search committee members present themselves and represent the institution will become part of each candidate's decision, should you make the candidate an offer. Further, the way you treat candidates will affect their impressions about the search and the institution that they will relate to others. Keeping this in mind, the following are key factors that could be deal-breakers for the candidates.

Staying on Schedule. Set your itinerary for the campus interview and stick to it, following the time frames indicated. Not only will staying on schedule ensure that all the stakeholders whose opinions you value will get a chance to meet the candidates without stress, it is also likely that the candidates will be impressed by your adherence to a schedule planned just for them.

Attending to Appearances. The college campus can be a place with varied dress codes for faculty, staff, and students. Professors in the business school may wear suits, while those in chemistry may wear blue jeans under their lab coats. Similarly, students may be dressed for an internship, or wearing their pajamas to morning classes. You can be sure that your candidates will look their professional best, and you should request that everyone involved in the search does as well. This is a sign of respect for the candidates and recognizes the importance of their visits. Casual faculty members may need to be reminded to dress for the occasion, and students may require guidance regarding professional (or, at least, business casual) attire and appearance.

It is also important to check the appearance of the meeting places and offices where the candidates will interview, present, eat lunch, and tour. At smaller schools like ours, we can call housekeeping and maintenance and request additional "TLC" in those areas. What ideas can you think of to ensure the school appears at its best for your guests' eyes?

Adhering to EEO/AA guidelines. During the process, don't lose sight of the training you conducted to avoid EEO/AA violations. Be sure to keep questions job related. Karen Gagie, Director of Human Resources at St. John Fisher College, also reminds search committee members to be sure their interviewing notes are brief, specific, and job related. They should not contain any personal or non–job-related topics.

Closing on a positive and powerful note. When you end the interview, be sure to indicate to your candidates where you are in the process and when they may expect to hear from you or the person charging the committee. Thank them for their interest in the college and their willingness to take the time to come for the interview, and assure them that you value their candidacy in this search process. Encourage them to contact you with any further questions or concerns. Additionally, as mentioned earlier, the contact person should follow up within a day or two after the interview to determine that the candidate arrived home safely and whether he or she had any additional questions.

Interviewing Beyond the Agenda

During the campus interview, the search committee needs to confirm the fit of the candidates for the college and the college for them. To this end, in addition to following your agenda, the committee may make additional notes about what happens between meetings, what reactions the candidates have to different situations, and any "red flags" that may appear. For example, one provost candidate in a recent search walked into each office on his campus tour and picked up all the literature that was available on the racks and tables, even though the search committee had provided him with a comprehensive information packet. Several people involved in the search noted that he showed active interest in the information the college communicated to its constituencies to aid in his decision process. Contrast this example with an internal faculty candidate who had no questions for the search committee. They took the lack of questions as a negative sign, that the candidate was not thinking through the changes involved in being an adjunct and moving into a tenure-track position.

Handling an Apparent "Misfit"

What happens if, shortly into the interview, you realize that this person isn't the right candidate for the job? Regardless of your personal observations, even if they are shared by other members of the search committee, you are still ethically obligated to continue with the entire interview schedule. It is unfair for a candidate who has prepared for this time to be sent home without completing the itinerary. It's also worth noting that, while some of those bad first impressions cannot be overcome, a candidate you find unacceptable may be acceptable to other campus constituencies. Others may even change your mind. We had one faculty candidate who did not make a good first impression because of her appearance and mannerisms. As the interview went on, however, she impressed us with her insight and knowledge of the position and the university, and we ended up making her the offer!

What if, shortly into the interview, the candidate tells you, "Look, I'm really not the person you're looking for to fill this position. It is best that I withdraw from the process"? While rare, this situation has occurred. Acknowledging that cases may differ, releasing the candidate from a pointless interview exercise may be in everyone's best interest. Consider following up with the candidate within a few days, when the emotional content of withdrawing has diminished, to ascertain what caused the decision to withdraw from the process. It is important to root out causes over which you have control—a discriminatory remark, a breach of confidentiality, or a negative first impression of someone or something on the campus, to name a few.

Troubleshooting the Unexpected

Whether you live in upstate New York, with ice storms, or Florida, with hurricanes, or California, with earthquakes and mudslides, weather can affect your best-laid interview plans. What other sorts of things may seriously impact a campus interview? Here is a partial list from our experiences:

- Candidate misses flight
- Candidate or key constituent has a death in the family
- Candidate's arrival is seriously disrupted or stalled due to weather
- Candidate is ill and cannot make the trip
- Candidate becomes ill after arrival
- Search committee member is ill and cannot make the interview
- Key constituent is ill and cannot make the interview
- Campus is without power due to ice storm or other emergency
- Candidate's luggage and presentation materials fail to arrive

We're sure that you can add others. Many things beyond your control can happen. However, if there is a change to the search process itinerary, you can do quick damage control if you consider the following:

- Keep in touch with the candidate about any changes in the schedule.
- Immediately notify all relevant constituencies about any change in plans. Use e-mail, a phone tree, or other search committee members to help contact affected parties.
- Make every effort to reschedule as quickly as possible.

You may also consider creative solutions to unexpected problems. For example, a local candidate may be able to return for a meeting with the ailing provost on another day. When one of our key constituents was ill, he did a phone interview with the candidate the following morning—and avoided exposing her to his germs!

Potential Pitfalls

- **Failure to confirm schedule and interview commitment with key constituencies**. This will be embarrassing to you and may compromise your search. Imagine bringing a faculty candidate to campus only to find the dean is out of town that day!
- **Not adhering to the planned time frame**. You will make a positive impression on your candidates by sticking to the schedule. It is also a courtesy to others involved in the search to maintain the planned time frame. Additionally, you risk missing some key constituencies if you run very late.
- **Not asking the planned questions.** This will become an issue as you evaluate your candidates. Key questions may remain unanswered, making it difficult to compare candidates.
- **Failing to maintain the confidentiality of the candidates.** It is crucial that everyone involved in any way be thoroughly briefed on the importance of confidentiality throughout, and even after, the search.
- **Allowing inappropriate questions or unseemly behavior from stakeholders.** Any individuals who participate in the interview process have the potential to impact the candidates' impressions of the institution. Their inappropriate behavior may be the tipping point for a desired candidate.
- **Ignoring basic principles of hospitality and hosting**. Candidates should always be treated as respected guests, which would include allowing the candidates some down time, opportunity to use the rest room, escort service to each appointment, and concern for their need for food and water.

Dealing with Internal Candidates

If an internal candidate is a finalist for a position, every effort must be taken to treat that candidate in the same way as the others. A similar itinerary should be followed and the same questions should be asked. You may dispense with the campus tour, but a visit to Human Resources is probably in order even for an internal candidate—for example, a faculty member who is applying for an administrative position will need information about the new benefits available. Internal candidates should not meet or be part of the interviews with any of the other candidates. We know of one search that was seriously compromised because an internal candidate attended presentations by the other candidates and participated in discussing their performances with members of the search committee. While EEO/AA laws do not protect internal candidates as a class, other guidelines for legal questioning must be followed during the interviews with internal candidates.

Checklist for the Campus Interview

- ❐ Scheduled meeting dates with search committee and other constituencies
- ❐ Scheduled and confirmed meetings with candidate
- ❐ Set itinerary for candidate meetings during visit
- ❐ Sent candidate informational packets prior to visit
- ❐ Sent contact person(s)' name and contact information to candidates
- ❐ Confirmed travel arrangements and sent information to candidate
- ❐ Notified candidate of their contact person
- ❐ Double-checked emergency contact system
- ❐ Notified housekeeping and maintenance—requested attention to meeting rooms
- ❐ Confirmed person greeting candidate and the time of candidate's arrival
- ❐ Assigned and confirmed escorts
- ❐ Made lunch reservations
- ❐ Followed agenda and stayed on time
- ❐ Followed interview protocol
- ❐ Responded quickly to reschedule any missed interviews due to unexpected incidents

CHAPTER 8

Evaluating the Finalists

In this chapter, you will

- Use a structured system to evaluate your top candidates
- Check references of the final candidates
- Incorporate feedback from diverse segments of the campus
- Work to reach consensus on a finalist or finalists
- Consider whether you need to acknowledge a failed search

Getting Started

THE EXCITEMENT is building. Now that each of the final candidates has spent time with you on campus, your favorites may be emerging. The tendency at this point is to persuade the other committee members of the wisdom of your preferred candidate and move the decision to a rapid conclusion. Practice patience—there are a few more steps to go! Reference checks, careful dialogue, and evaluation of all the information are especially important at this critical juncture in the process. Without them, you may precipitate a failed search or miss an exceptional candidate.

Evaluating and Prioritizing the Candidates

Immediately following the candidate interviews, each search committee member should complete an evaluation form for each finalist, documenting evidence of the search criteria and the factors that led to their conclusions. Evaluation forms come in myriad formats. Some search committees prefer a numeric rating system, some favor a strengths/weaknesses format, while others employ a hybrid of the two.

What might an individual search committee member's evaluation form for a candidate look like? An example of a hybrid format appears on pages 66–67.

Incorporating feedback from stakeholders

During this stage of the process, you will assimilate the feedback you received from other campus constituencies and the references. Because you used a systematic form, the information is organized and focused on the qualities and behaviors important to you. It eliminates the time-consuming tedium of reading through disparate notes and e-mails and allows you to compile rather quickly a list of comments based on the qualities you identified as important in the new hire.

An example of feedback on two candidates who met with a group of ten students, after it was collected and compiled, appears on pages 68.

It is clear from the student feedback that Dr. Wallace made a more positive impression on the students than Dr. Grommet. They were impressed by Dr. Wallace's personality, and that came through in their evaluations. Because students are an important constituency for faculty members, their feedback must be considered. At the same time, student feedback alone should not dictate hiring recommendations.

However, there is one level of feedback that may outweigh the opinions of the committee members—serious reservations voiced by the person who charged

Candidate Interview Evaluation: Dean of Engineering

Applicant's Name: *Dr. Michael Keester*

Interviewer's Name: *Barb Dwyer*

Key Background Review

Educational background

Tenured faculty member. Experience with curriculum development. Continues to teach an occasional graduate course. Seems to understand needs in classroom.
Asked good questions about our core curriculum—seemed to identify some of the problems we've been wrestling with.

Administrative background

Chaired large Electrical Engineering department—25 f/t faculty, graduate program. Developed new program in computer engineering.
Some concern about budget administration—had a lot of support in this area.

The Critical Dimensions

Faculty Hiring and Development

Good experience with engineering faculty. Tried to diversify faculty in lean budget times—moderately successful. Brought in 2 women to faculty.

Program Development

Began new computer engineering program. Relatively new program; success of venture unclear at this time.

Assessment

Experienced with accrediting agencies' requirements. Led faculty team for Middle States' evaluation in '02. Successful outcome. Some success with assessment throughout department but not a consistent effort.

Diversity Characteristics to Consider

Candidate does not fit diversity profile, but worked to diversify his own faculty in last position.

Candidate's Questions

Note the questions here:

1. *Asked about the process for changing core curriculum.*
2. *Seemed concerned about why position was open.*
3. *What problems did we faculty see as the major challenges to the university?*
4. *Asked about new program development and expansion into graduate programs.*

Rating

For each dimension, check the box that most accurately describes your rating of the candidate on that dimension.

Dimensions	Exceptional 5	Above Standard (4)	Standard 3	Below Standard (2)	Unacceptable 1
1. Educational Background		X			
2. Administrative Experience		X			
3. Program Development			X		
4. Budget Administration				X	
5. Faculty Hiring and Development	X				
6. Teamwork Skills	X				
7. Accreditation Experience	X				
8. Information Technology Experience			X		

Comments:

Total: *31/40*

Overall Evaluation

Taking into account all the relevant information you have obtained in this interview, what is your overall evaluation of this candidate?

Exceptional ____ Above Standard *X* Standard ____ Below Standard ____ Unacceptable ____

Rank compared to other candidates: *2*

Student Evaluations of Lunch Meeting 2-14

History Department Faculty Candidate: Dr. J. Wallace

Dimensions	Exceptional	Above Average	Good	Below Average	Unable to Judge
1. Teaching Demonstration	8	2			
2. Academic Advising			3		7
3. Career Counseling		5	5		
4. History Club Advisor	4	6			

Other comments:

- a good listener
- asked us a lot of questions, we didn't get to ask all of ours
- a real expert in the field
- likes softball, could play on our team

Student Evaluations of Lunch Meeting 2-14

History Department Faculty Candidate: Dr. H. Grommet

Dimensions	Exceptional	Above Average	Good	Below Average	Unable to Judge
1. Teaching Demonstration			2	8	
2. Academic Advising				4	6
3. Career Counseling		10			
4. History Club Advisor		2	5	3	

Other comments:

- so nervous, I was distracted during the class
- knows a lot about the field but doesn't seem comfortable around students
- answered questions very briefly

the committee or a higher level administrator. The committee needs to take those comments into account in its final recommendation.

Checking References

References should be checked before extending an offer to the final candidate. The reason for checking references is predicated on the belief that past performance predicts future performance. Beyond verifying the information from the candidate's resumé, search committees use reference checks to clarify, corroborate, and assess the abilities, skills, personal fit and other qualifications presented by the candidates. You may conduct the checks yourselves, delegate the task to the Human Resources department, or outsource them to a contracted service. One advantage of doing the checks yourselves is relevance. Because you have interacted with the candidates rather closely, you may find it enlightening to speak with people who know them and their work. You will be better able to probe for additional information in areas of concern than someone who has not met the candidate.

To ensure that you obtain relevant information, it's important to plan your approach, prepare pointed questions, and elicit in-depth information in your conversations with the reference givers.

Whose references do you check? This depends on whether your institution has specific guidelines for reference checking during the search process. The policy at the University of Florida, for example, is that references for all finalists must be checked, regardless of whether the final candidate is an external applicant or internal university employee. Unless your institution has a specific requirement, we recommend that you check the references only of those who are finalists for your position. Spending time checking references for candidates whose applications will not be pursued beyond the initial screening or phone interview takes valuable time. Additionally, the process of checking references discloses some information about your search process and your candidates, and this should be kept to a minimum to protect the confidentiality of the search and the candidates.

Planning Your Approach

At the very beginning, decide what kind of information you need, how you're going to solicit it, and from whom. It's critical that everyone representing the search committee is clearly instructed that the purpose is to gather factual information on the candidate through descriptions and illustrative examples, not opinions or speculations.

Selecting People to Contact

Start with the candidate's list of references but remember that savvy candidates carefully select and prepare their reference givers. They want to present themselves in the most positive light for the position, so be sure that their list includes at least one person who managed them, one person who worked closely with them, and if appropriate, someone who reported to them. It's important to talk with people who have had the opportunity to observe the candidate in action. Try to get names of people who will provide balanced yet diverse perspectives. A rule of thumb is to check at least three references from the candidate's list whose contact has been within the past five to seven years. Because you want examples and factual information, reference relationships that are ten or more years old are fairly useless. For obvious reasons, you should not accept references from friends, relatives, or persons who have not had the opportunity to observe job-related performance. We have also found it very informative to speak in depth with students who interacted with our candidates. These conversations reveal insights that cannot be gleaned through the structured evaluations forms they filled out.

Smart reference checkers also inquire of the primary reference givers: "Do you know anyone else who could add to our perspective about this candidate?" This is one way of breaking out of the trap of talking only to the candidate's champions. Ask for the names of co-workers or colleagues who were not on their list. These contacts can round out your picture of the candidate and may provide an insight about any discrepancies you may uncover.

However, it might be wise to check with Human Resources to be certain this is acceptable practice. Arizona State University, for example, directs its search committees to be consistent in their treatment of candidates when unsolicited reference information (i.e., the person providing the information is not on the candidate's reference list) is made available either through direct knowledge or through the provision of the information by another individual. For example, if search committee members have direct knowledge of a specific candidate or receive unsolicited information, all members must either share this information for all candidates or not share such information about any candidate.

The search committee would also be wise to obtain consent from the candidate before contacting references. Most Human Resources offices supply consent or waiver forms. While you want to honor the candidate's request for confidentiality and do not wish to put their current employment in jeopardy, this must not deter you from speaking with appropriate references when the candidate is a finalist for the position.

Developing Questions that Elicit Behaviors

Sound familiar? It is! You can use the behavioral interviewing technique described in chapter 5 to elicit incidents and examples that are relevant to the position. By asking for stories, you will learn the particulars of the situations or tasks that the candidate faced, the choices they made, and the impact of their actions. Your questions, obviously, must pertain to the position. You must be vigilant about avoiding illegal questions. Appropriate areas of inquiry include:

- Job responsibilities
- Quality of overall job performance
- Productivity
- Ability to work with others
- Strengths
- Weaknesses
- Areas for improvement
- Specific achievements on the job
- Motivation
- Eligibility for rehire

In addition, the reference check needs to include the verification of all degrees. According to industry experts, one-third of all resumés and applications contain material falsehoods. One of the most common deceptions is claiming to hold a degree that was never conferred. In a recent news story in upstate New York, a candidate for a school superintendent's position was found to have purchased a Ph.D. from a degree mill in England. Don't take a document or copy of it at face value. Instead, confirm the credential with the college or university registrar's office.

Preparing for the Call

Organize the information you want to elicit. We like to use a checklist to remind ourselves of the information we're seeking, present our prepared questions in an orderly and logical sequence, and record notes about the responses from the reference giver to each of the questions.

A simple reference checklist appears on page 71.

In preparation for the reference checks, you should also develop questions based on the critical dimensions for the position. Behavioral event questions are well suited to this situation since the references will be in an excellent position to provide specific examples. Here are a few examples:

- ***Teaching:*** How would you describe [Candidate's] teaching style? Can you think of a time when [Candidate] faced some significant challenges in the classroom and how he worked to overcome those challenges?
- ***Advising:*** How would you describe [Candidate's] one-on-one interaction with students? This position includes being the pre-med advisor. What specific experience does [Candidate] have in counseling students who are planning to attend medical school?
- ***Collaboration:*** What experience did [Candidate] have working in teams at your institution? Did she do any collaborative research with other faculty across departments?

Conduct your reference checks in person or by phone. While it may seem expedient to use e-mail or correspondence, these methods present many drawbacks. You are not able to ask follow-up questions or inquire about hesitancies, inconsistencies, or reservations that may be implied if not spoken. In addition, confidentiality could be compromised by using electronic communication.

Conducting the Reference Check

The following steps, adapted from the Canadian Public Service Commission website (www.psc-cfp.gc.ca) provide an excellent guide for conducting fruitful checks:

1. **Be thoroughly familiar with the candidate's file.** Just before you contact the reference giver, review the candidate's information, such as notes from interviews, previous reference checks, or the candidate's resumé.
2. **Open the call with an explanation of who you are and why you're calling.** Explain the responsibilities of the position the candidate

Phone Reference Check

Date: ______________________________

Position: ______________________________

Name of Candidate: ______________________________

Name and Title of Reference: ______________________________

Phone #: ______________________________

Name of person conducting reference check: ______________________________

1. Verify dates of employment: ______________________________
2. Verify position: ______________________________
3. Overall, how did [Candidate] handle the position?

   ____

   ____

   ____

4. Were there any issues that affected [Candidate's] ability to do the job?

   ____

   ____

   ____

5. What was [Candidate's] reason for leaving this position?

   ____

   ____

   ____

6. Would you rehire [Candidate]? ______ yes ______ no
7. Is there anything else you would like to add?

   ____

   ____

   ____

   ____

is pursuing and your desire for relevant information to qualify the candidate. Do not say that the candidate "has been selected" for the position; say instead that the candidate "is being considered."

3. **Follow your plan**. This allows you to follow up on relevant but unexpected pieces of information without getting distracted. Begin with verifying the basic information such as job title, functions, salary, and dates of employment.
4. **Sort out opinions from facts and examples**. Remember, your aim is to collect facts, observations, and examples. Take note of opinions but pursue the specific observations, facts, and incidents on which the opinions are based.
5. **Write down as much as you can**. Detailed notes will be important later when you evaluate the information, and they will guide you during the reference check process as you formulate follow-up questions.
6. **Collect relevant information without evaluating it.** Save the evaluation for after the phone call or meeting.
7. **Be alert to**:
   - Unusual hesitations
   - Ambiguous or evasive responses
   - Overly negative or vindictive responses
   - Overly enthusiastic responses

   If you get the impression that a reference giver is not being completely frank with you, take note. You may wish to return to the topic later or explore it with another reference person.
8. **Take the time you need**. If the reference giver is pressed for time, suggest continuing the conversation at a more convenient time.
9. **Express appreciation.** Thank the reference giver for providing a valuable service to you and the institution. Leave your name and number in case the person wants to call you back.
10. **If warranted, re-contact the reference person.** This may be appropriate if information from a subsequent contact reveals some inconsistencies or important aspects that were missed.

Evaluating the Information

It is the search committee's responsibility to evaluate the relevance of the information and to use it intelligently. It's your responsibility to put different sources of information into the proper perspective and to make a final determination for your own needs. Don't take all reference check information at face value. Consider the reasons why some information may not fit with the rest. Is the reference giver withholding negative information? Does he or she want to get rid of an unproductive employee? Is the person afraid of a libel suit? Has the person been told by his or her institution not to give references? Be wary of giving undue weight to isolated incidents. Rather, look for patterns of behavior.

When you have checked the references of each of the finalists, weigh the information in the same manner for all candidates. What disqualifies one should be the basis for disqualifying any other.

In the end, references are only one piece of the search process puzzle. Your final decision about the candidate must be derived from a reasoned synthesis of all the information you have gathered from all of the sources.

Deciding on the Candidates to Recommend

The decision on the candidates to recommend should be made after careful and thorough consideration of all the information, the assessments of each of the committee members, feedback from references, and an informed dialogue among the members at a meeting in which all are present. Calling the meeting to evaluate the finalists and choose the final candidates is an exciting point in the process and a critical step. It needs to be managed well by the chair in order for the goals of the search committee to be met.

The tendency at this point is to want to make a quick decision. It's common for members to promote their favorite candidate with the hope that the others agree and the decision is swift and painless. While advocating for a candidate is a key factor, weighing the evidence of the candidates' strengths against the needs of the department, the charge to the committee, and the voices of the stakeholders are essential factors in the process. It may take some time. In our experience, the time is well spent. The role of the chair is to call and conduct the meeting in a manner that will ensure that everyone's

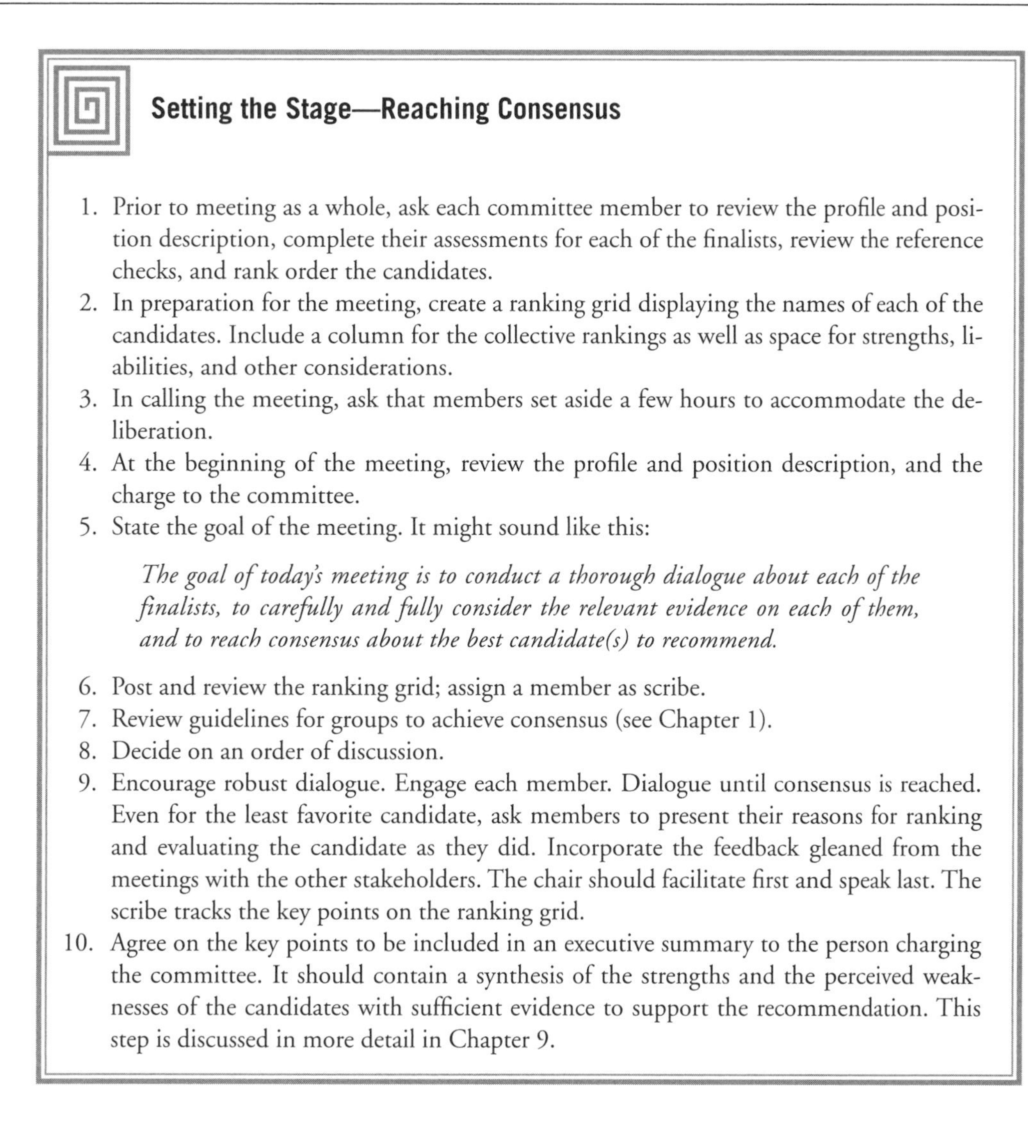

Setting the Stage—Reaching Consensus

1. Prior to meeting as a whole, ask each committee member to review the profile and position description, complete their assessments for each of the finalists, review the reference checks, and rank order the candidates.
2. In preparation for the meeting, create a ranking grid displaying the names of each of the candidates. Include a column for the collective rankings as well as space for strengths, liabilities, and other considerations.
3. In calling the meeting, ask that members set aside a few hours to accommodate the deliberation.
4. At the beginning of the meeting, review the profile and position description, and the charge to the committee.
5. State the goal of the meeting. It might sound like this:

   The goal of today's meeting is to conduct a thorough dialogue about each of the finalists, to carefully and fully consider the relevant evidence on each of them, and to reach consensus about the best candidate(s) to recommend.

6. Post and review the ranking grid; assign a member as scribe.
7. Review guidelines for groups to achieve consensus (see Chapter 1).
8. Decide on an order of discussion.
9. Encourage robust dialogue. Engage each member. Dialogue until consensus is reached. Even for the least favorite candidate, ask members to present their reasons for ranking and evaluating the candidate as they did. Incorporate the feedback gleaned from the meetings with the other stakeholders. The chair should facilitate first and speak last. The scribe tracks the key points on the ranking grid.
10. Agree on the key points to be included in an executive summary to the person charging the committee. It should contain a synthesis of the strengths and the perceived weaknesses of the candidates with sufficient evidence to support the recommendation. This step is discussed in more detail in Chapter 9.

voice is heard. The consensus process outlined on this page has worked well for us.

Potential Pitfall: Evaluating the "Fit" for the Campus

Christian's Story

A few years ago, I was involved in a search for a high level administrator. The finalists were two well-known and highly respected local candidates and one out-of-town candidate whom some of the committee members had been reluctant to invite because he wasn't perceived as a fit for the culture. However, after the interviews, when the evaluation forms were being completed, the strength of the out-of-town candidate began to emerge. In the dialogue during the decision meeting, different committee members highlighted a variety of strengths that were not present as robustly or as fully developed in the heretofore preferred candidates. These strengths, when coupled with very strong impressions voiced by the constituencies who had shared an informal meal with him and attended his presentation, solidified the "dark horse" as our candidate of choice. He was offered and enthusiastically accepted the appointment.

Even at this late stage, be careful to not to eliminate a candidate as a poor fit based on a different look, a different approach, or an unconventional research agenda. It is tempting to eliminate a candidate that we think won't be a "good fit" for the college based on the way the position has been filled in the past. The committee needs to look carefully at its criteria for evaluation to be sure it isn't passing up an opportunity to diversify the campus.

Additionally, Vice President and Chief Legal Counsel Jonathan Alger of Rutgers University notes that "the use of collegiality as a separate, free-standing criterion in hiring and promotion cases has been called into question, particularly since it can easily become a smokescreen for subtle forms of discrimination" (personal communication, 11-18-04). The American Association of University Professors provides a good resource on this subject as well as others related to hiring from a diverse candidate pool.

Acknowledging a Failed Search

Mary's Story

Our search committee had conducted in-depth on-campus interviews with five semifinalists for the faculty position. At the conclusion of the process, two emerged as the strongest finalists. We met to rank order the finalists to send their names on to the Provost. The discussion included a compilation of the committee members' own rankings as well as feedback we had collected from other constituencies, primarily students who studied in that academic area. As we discussed the finalists, we began to realize that, while each had his strengths and one was a minority candidate, neither would be acceptable to the current Provost. During the search process, a new Provost had been hired at the institution, and her ideas for this position differed significantly from what the search committee had originally envisioned. While both of our finalists were good teachers, neither had the degree and scholarship needed to satisfy the new Provost. Our search committee had a hint of this when we heard a rumor about a failed search in another department, but, in our desire to get the hiring done, we proceeded with the search. As we approached the conclusion of the process, we realized our mistake. We declared a failed search. A new search was inaugurated in the summer using a position description revised in consultation with the new Provost.

After diligently working through eight steps of a systematic process, it is difficult to face the possibility of a "failed search." The prospect of not being able to fill a vacancy in the anticipated time frame and starting over with a new process can be frustrating and demoralizing. On the other hand, when you refuse to "settle" for a candidate who doesn't meet the needs of the department or the institution, you uphold the credibility and integrity of the search. At the same time you enable the department to better meet its needs in the long run by providing new perspectives by which it can align its priorities. What are some of the reasons for declaring a search "failed"? Here are a few from our experience:

- No qualified candidates applied for the position.
- The committee did not meet its diversity goals in the hiring process.
- The integrity of the process was compromised by a breach of confidentiality or use of inappropriate strategies.
- No acceptable candidates emerged from the process.
- The search committee could not agree on the candidates to recommend.
- The person charging the committee was dissatisfied with the finalists.
- The requirements for the job changed during the course of the search.
- The finalist turned the job down and none of the other candidates was acceptable.

Regardless of the reason, the reality is that the position remains open. The next move is the prerogative of the person who originally charged the committee. One decision maker will re-start the search process immediately with the same search committee. Another will reconstitute the search committee and appoint new members. Still another may ask the search committee to suggest a temporary solution to cover the vacancy until the search is re-opened. In the case cited above, the committee recommended giving a one-year contract to an experienced adjunct while they searched for a person to fill the tenure-track position.

When a search is re-opened, the search committee needs to return to the original position description to assess whether a flaw in the early stages of the process may have led to the failure of the first search. The current state of the field should be re-researched and stakeholders re-interviewed to be sure that no important information has been overlooked.

Reference

Affirmative Action Plans (1983). American Association of University Professors, Retrieved 02/24/05 from www.aaup.org/statements/Redbook/AARD PLAN.HTM

Checklist for Evaluating the Finalists

- ❒ Completed individual evaluation forms on each finalist
- ❒ Checked references in a systematic way for each finalist
- ❒ Evaluated and incorporated feedback from constituencies
- ❒ Dialogued to reach consensus on a final candidate or candidates

CHAPTER 9

Negotiating and Making the Offer

In this chapter, you will

- Prepare to present the finalist(s) to the person charging the committee
- Create a case by gathering appropriate information and writing a compelling narrative
- Anticipate family/partner issues
- Close the loop with other candidates in the process
- Complete paperwork needed for Human Resources and/or the diversity officer
- Evaluate your process
- Celebrate a job well done!

Getting Started

CONGRATULATIONS! You have determined the final candidate or candidates for your open position. This is an exciting moment for you, the finalist, and the person who charged the search. All of you want to make the best decision for the candidate and the institution. The importance of handling the negotiation of the offer in a masterful way cannot be underestimated. A highly desired candidate could be lost at this stage if it is not handled well. The good news is that at most institutions, the search committee is not directly involved with the negotiation of the offer. The bad news is that you could lose an outstanding candidate by not seeking out and sharing information you possess with the decision maker.

During the search and interview process, search committee members have enjoyed extended contact with each candidate. Your task now is to prepare a compelling case for hiring the candidate or candidates of choice from the points of view of both the candidate and the institution. As you prepare the presentation of the finalists' credentials and strengths, also prepare a best-case scenario of the critical hiring factors for each of them. This step increases the chances that the candidate of choice will accept a reasonable offer.

Preparing to Present the Finalists to the Decision Maker

In charging the search committee, the hiring authority specified whether one or more finalists should be presented and whether they should be presented in priority order. In most searches, the decision maker is presented with two or three final candidates to choose from. The committee prepares a brief but compelling case for each candidate that encompasses the candidate's strengths and unique selling points for the position, weaknesses and deficits, any concerns, and an assessment of what it would take to get the candidate.

In order to do this, you need to create a compelling case for your top candidate.

Distinguishing Compelling Conditions to Attract the Candidate

Having talked with each of the final candidates informally as well as having interviewed them, the next step is to ask, "What would it take for us to get this candidate?" Begin by compiling the collective information from your various contacts with the candidate. Next, review the feedback you received from the constituents who interviewed the candidate on campus. If any of your finalists is a referred candidate, call the referring person and ask his or her opinion about what it would take to get the candidate. In checking the candidate's references, ask the reference givers for their opinions about the drivers and rewards that are likely to attract the candidate.

In many institutions, the Human Resources department researches and substantiates the competitive salary information for the level of the position and benchmarks against comparable institutions. HR guides the decision maker through the salary negotiation; in some institutions HR may actually extend and negotiate the offer. However, the search committee might compile some comparative data from comparable institutions to offer additional benchmarks and recommendations for the final negotiations.

Recognizing that there are numerous aspects to an offer and multiple factors that contribute to a candidate accepting your offer, you might include features such as those shown in the table below in addition to compensation.

Your Role in the Negotiating Process

While you will probably not be privy to the details of the offer made to the candidate of choice, your role is to help the decision maker convert the candidate to a hire. During this stage in the process, a member of the search committee, typically the committee chair, may be contacted by the candidate seeking additional information to inform his or her decision. We have found that it is especially important at this stage to communicate that the candidate is wanted and to demonstrate in action and affect that the process is sincere and aboveboard. Be as responsive as you can to the candidate, and, at the same time, keep the decision maker fully informed of your interactions. The candidate's concerns and requests illuminate the critical issues affecting her or his decision, and by conveying the candidate's concerns, you enable the decision maker to address them in a proactive manner.

Potential Pitfall: Failing to Make a Case for Your Candidate

Renate's Story

I was chairing a search to hire a new director of the campus writing center. At the conclusion of our process, I scheduled a meeting with the dean to ask him how he wanted to proceed on making the decision and extending the offer. I was caught off guard when he said, "Who do you like best?" I said, "We like Jim." He answered, "Good, so do I. I'll go ahead and make the offer." His attention turned to other business on his desk and I was out of the office in less than five minutes. As I walked back to my office, I had a sinking feeling about the offer. I wished that I had been more assertive about the issues we knew were important to Jim.

The following week the Dean called. He told me that Jim had declined the offer. I was shocked and dismayed. When I asked about the reason, the Dean replied, "He felt the offer was too low." That's when I realized that I should have insisted on sharing our findings about Jim with the Dean. There were other factors beyond the salary that were important to Jim, but how would the Dean have known to include them?

In Renate's situation, the search committee had the most thorough knowledge of their candidate of choice and the best information about what it would take to get the candidate to accept an offer. In contrast, the Dean's image of the candidate was incomplete, based only on the resumé and a one-hour meeting.

Features that might contribute to a candidate's acceptance of an offer

Teaching/work load	Relocation expenses	Spousal employment assistance
Tenure	Professional development	Support assistance
Timing of promotions	Sponsorship in professional organizations	Training
Equipment	Travel allowance	Housing assistance

What could the search committee have done to make the Dean's job easier and increase the likelihood that the offer would be accepted? We recommend that the search committee prepare a presentation of the final candidates for the decision maker.

The presentation to the decision maker can be made in a number of ways, depending on your institution. In some places, a written narrative is actually required for the presentation of the finalists and becomes part of the retained record for the search. Other schools ask only for a face-to-face meeting with the person who charged the committee. Still others use a combination of the two methods. When an oral presentation is requested, we recommend that you at least prepare a review or summary sheet on each candidate, to remind the decision maker of the most crucial strengths and weaknesses of each.

Whether in writing or in person, it is important that you make a strong and thoughtful case for your candidate(s) of choice. Be balanced in your presentation of assets and liabilities, and address key areas of the profile that you thought helped this candidate make it to finalist status.

The examples on this page and the next show what such a narrative for the decision maker might look like.

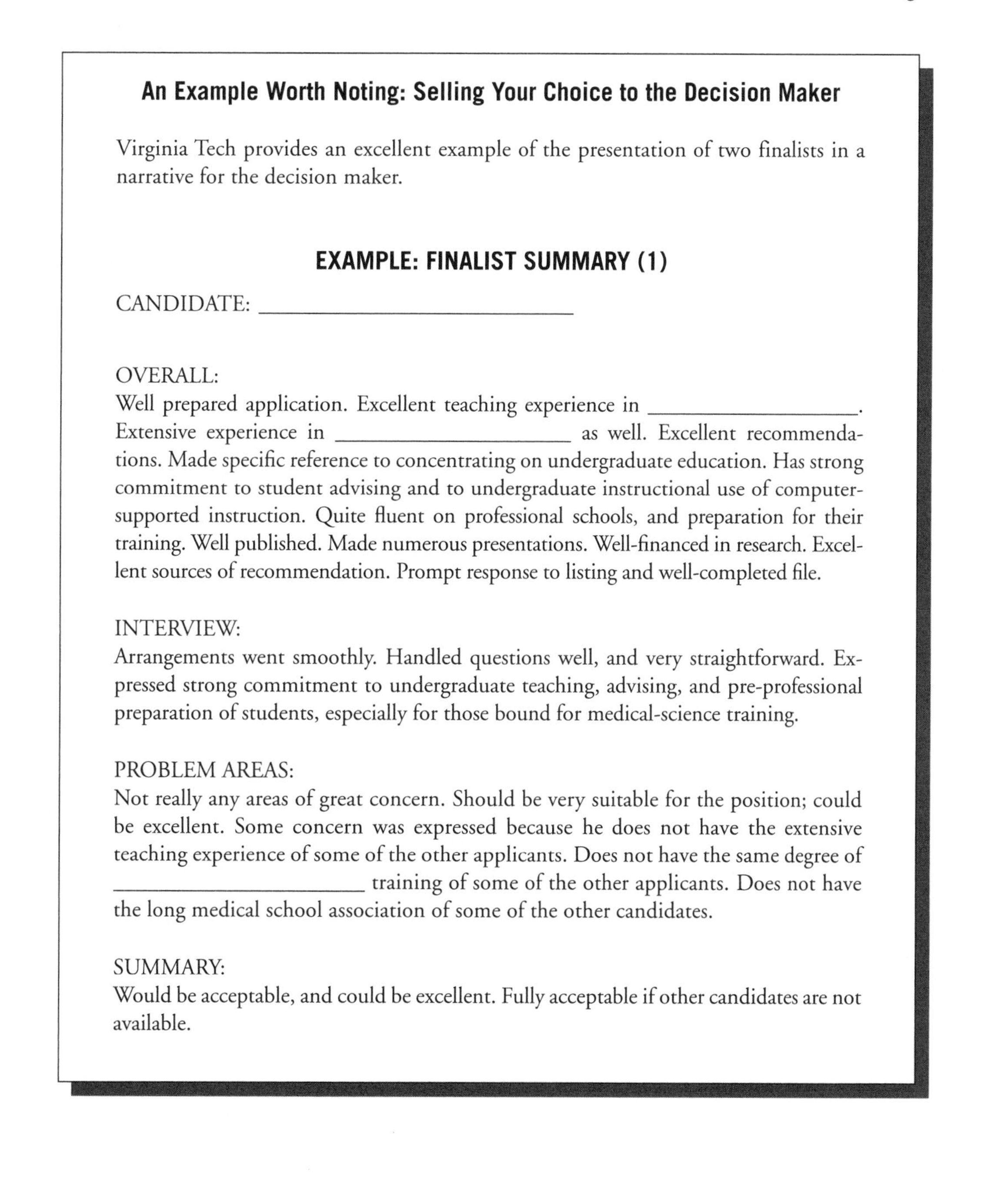

An Example Worth Noting: Selling Your Choice to the Decision Maker

Virginia Tech provides an excellent example of the presentation of two finalists in a narrative for the decision maker.

EXAMPLE: FINALIST SUMMARY (1)

CANDIDATE: ____________________

OVERALL:
Well prepared application. Excellent teaching experience in ______________. Extensive experience in ________________ as well. Excellent recommendations. Made specific reference to concentrating on undergraduate education. Has strong commitment to student advising and to undergraduate instructional use of computer-supported instruction. Quite fluent on professional schools, and preparation for their training. Well published. Made numerous presentations. Well-financed in research. Excellent sources of recommendation. Prompt response to listing and well-completed file.

INTERVIEW:
Arrangements went smoothly. Handled questions well, and very straightforward. Expressed strong commitment to undergraduate teaching, advising, and pre-professional preparation of students, especially for those bound for medical-science training.

PROBLEM AREAS:
Not really any areas of great concern. Should be very suitable for the position; could be excellent. Some concern was expressed because he does not have the extensive teaching experience of some of the other applicants. Does not have the same degree of ________________ training of some of the other applicants. Does not have the long medical school association of some of the other candidates.

SUMMARY:
Would be acceptable, and could be excellent. Fully acceptable if other candidates are not available.

EXAMPLE: FINALIST SUMMARY (2)

CANDIDATE: ___________________________

OVERALL:
Well prepared application. Excellent teaching experience in ____________________. Excellent recommendations. Excellent student evaluations. Well published. Excellent and relevant research experience. Numerous presentations as the result of many years of postdoctoral research. Prompt response, and well completed file. Appeared very intelligent, which is borne out in his recommendations. Very organized. Excellent contacts at both CSU and USHSC. High achiever.

INTERVIEW:
Appeared very sharp. Organized. Handled questions well, but very terse. Had an excellent grasp of field of ____________________. Open. Honest.

PROBLEM AREAS:
Two of the three interviewers didn't evaluate him as high as the other candidates. Part of the problem may have been due to a (possible) mix-up in arrangements, or his admitted inexperience in the interview process. He did not come across as being truly interested in the position or the college. When asked (standard question) why he wanted to come to the university, his entire response centered on personal and familial reasons. THERE WAS NO COMMENT MADE AS TO THE GOALS AND STUDENTS of Virginia Tech. When asked about his professional goals, he expressed the thought of moving into administration fairly soon. There was real concern about his ability to identify and communicate with "general studies" students, given his background in teaching upper division and ________ courses. He claimed to be able to bridge this gap—the writer was not convinced. THIS POSITION HEAVILY EMPHASIZES GENERAL STUDIES EDUCATION. There certainly was the question of whether he was truly interested in the university and its goals, or more interested in staying in Blacksburg, where his home and (extended) family is. It may have been the circumstances, but there seemed to be a degree of arrogance to the person that made some of us very uncomfortable, and raised the question of how he would interact with the department and general studies students.

SUMMARY:
A very bright, very confident, very well-qualified individual. Very strong recommendations. Real concerns about his commitment to "hard core teaching" (this is a hard core teaching position, at least for a few years), his ability to identify with "Virginia Tech students." His manner and comments did not reduce these concerns one bit!

Making the Offer

Once a top candidate for the position has been identified, it is time for the formal offer to be made. Most often, this is done by the person who charged the committee. However, sometimes this task is delegated to the chair of the search committee or Human Resources.

In our experience, the initial offer in academia is normally made by phone contact with the candidate. We prefer to send the candidate an e-mail asking when he or she might be available for a phone conversation. This enables you to give them a hint of what might be coming, so you don't catch them off guard or in an awkward situation at their current position. Most candidates will arrange a time when they can be at home to receive the call in relative privacy.

After the phone conversation, in which the specifics of the offer are presented, Human Resources or the office of the person who charged the committee mails out a formal contract or letter. The candidate is generally given a date by which the contract must be signed and returned or the offer is declared void.

Because candidates may be balancing multiple offers, every effort should be made to give them adequate time to make their decision, while not compromising your need to fill the position with a solid candidate (even if that person is your second choice). During this decision time, candidates may also need to negotiate some aspects of the offer. This is generally done directly with the person who charged the committee. Beyond the specific job offer, candidates may have other concerns that need to be addressed. We discuss one of the most common and significant concerns in the next section.

Anticipating Family/Partner Issues

During the negotiation process, the final candidates face the reality that the choice they make will affect their families as well as their careers. For finalists who divulge their marital/partner/family situations, it is important that you acknowledge the key note they play in the decision. The candidate's spouse or significant other surely plays a key role in that decision. A wise committee extends an invitation to the partner to visit the campus, tour the area, look at neighborhoods, meet other partners, and connect to resources of personal and professional interest to them. It's important to present the advantages of the move to the partner as well as to the final candidate.

In a recent search for a division head, the search committee learned that the spouse of the candidate of choice was a weaver. Prior to her visit, care was taken to gather information about the local weaver's guild in the area. When she visited the campus, the search committee presented the information to her, introduced her to a staff member who shared her interest in weaving, and instructed the real estate agent showing her housing choices to take her to a suburb where sheep could be raised. The partner was impressed with the extent of the weaving resources in the area; however, she was even more impressed with the expressed concern for her assimilation. She became an ally in her spouse's choice to accept the offer even though the compensation was lower than they had desired.

Closing the Loop with Other Candidates and Referring Parties

When the candidate of choice accepts and signs the offer, the search is concluded. It is time for the committee to notify the candidates in process and those on hold. It's very important that you carefully and accurately document the process that led to the final offer. Update your database and indicate the outcome for each candidate. It is also recommended that the committee personally inform each person who referred a candidate about the outcome, especially in the case of the finalists. By demonstrating the integrity of the search process, you can greatly enhance the reputation of your school among peers. The word spreads among colleagues and interested parties that yours is an institution that treats candidates with respect and communicates the selection process clearly and candidly.

While e-mail is currently used for a great deal of business correspondence, we strongly suggest that you send a personal letter to each of the finalists and referring parties and that you personalize the information for each candidate. See the example on page 82.

Even though you "close the loop" with the deselected finalists in the search, there may be reasons to keep them "alive" as potential candidates for other searches at your school. In a search for a dean of students, we took note of a very good candidate who had been eliminated because, in comparison to the other finalists, she was not as strong. However, the college was also searching for a director of residential life, a position for which this individual seemed well suited. We referred her to that search committee, which interviewed her, and she was hired. Moreover, our instincts that she was an exceptional candidate have been corroborated by her subsequent career moves. She went on to earn both a Ph.D. and an Executive MBA while working full time, and today she is vice president for student affairs at a major research institution in the Northeast.

Rejection Letter for Finalist

Dear Dr. Denton:

The English Department enjoyed meeting you during your visit to our campus to interview for Director of the Campus Writing Center. We especially appreciated the time and effort you put into developing a writing workshop on "The Use of the Comma," which was very well received by the faculty and the senior students.

The Search Committee has had a difficult challenge—choosing a final candidate from among the outstanding four finalists, of which you were one. You were highly competitive and very well received by our faculty and students. In the end, we selected another candidate who has accepted our offer. Although we regret that we are not able to offer you a position at this time, we plan to retain your resumé in the event that another opportunity opens in the near future.

In the meantime, we wish you much success in your career endeavors.

Sincerely,

Phyllis Steen
Chair, Search Committee

Completing the Paperwork

This is the point in the process when the chair ensures that the forms required by your Human Resources, Diversity, or Affirmative Action offices are completed. Our experience has shown that state and public universities generally require more detailed information and record keeping on the applicants than private colleges. The rating form you used throughout the process provides all the data generally needed to compile the tally form for the official records. A typical tally form may look like the one on page 83.

Completing the tally of candidates also contributes to evaluating the search process, as described in the next section.

Shedding and Shredding

At the conclusion of the search, the chair needs to be sure there is one complete set of resumés, cover letters, minutes from search committee meetings including votes, all correspondence and reference checks, and other supporting materials for every applicant involved in the process. This set should be retained for a minimum of two years from the date of appointment of the candidate. Beyond this one complete set, members of the search committee and other constituents must shred or permanently dispose of all other documentation, including any resumés that may have been distributed to other constituencies involved in the process. Remember, resumés and cover letters are confidential documents. They contain sensitive informa-

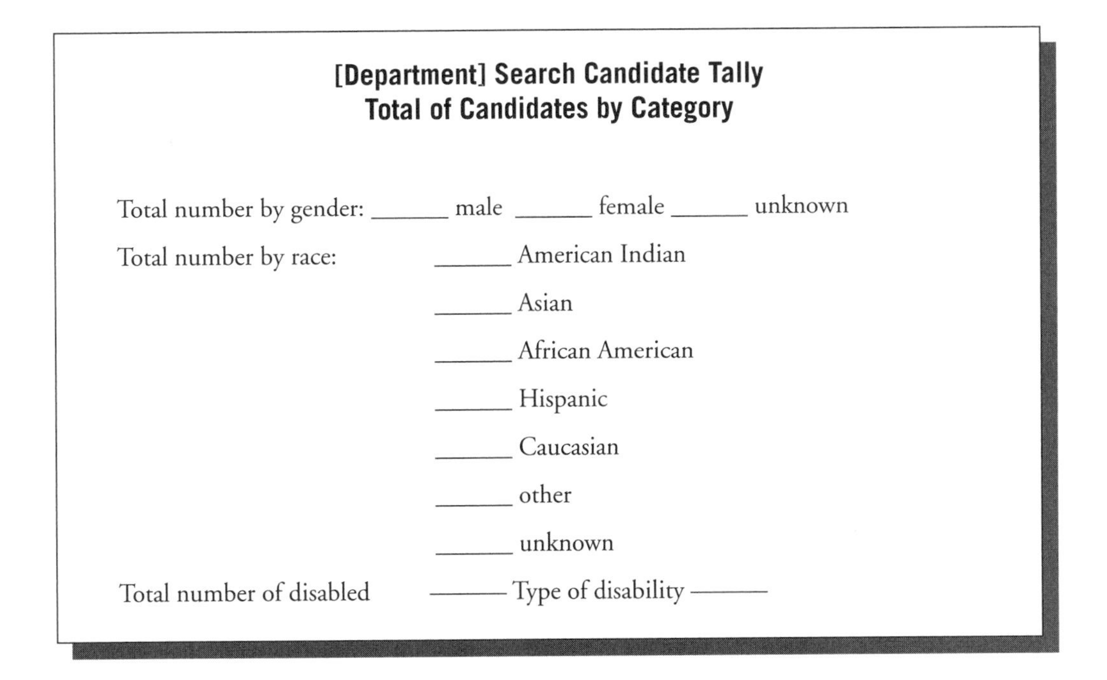

[Department] Search Candidate Tally
Total of Candidates by Category

Total number by gender: ______ male ______ female ______ unknown

Total number by race: ______ American Indian
______ Asian
______ African American
______ Hispanic
______ Caucasian
______ other
______ unknown

Total number of disabled ______ Type of disability ______

tion and, in the case of those who did not receive or accept the position, divulging their applications may violate their privacy.

Doing the Numbers and Evaluating the Process

The search committee, the decision maker, and HR all have a vested interest in the outcome of the search. Your database is the source for counting the EEO/AA numbers. How many male and female candidates? What about finalists? How many ethnic minorities, by gender, were moved to the second and third round interviews? Did you attract disabled applicants? What happened to them in the process? It's enlightening to look at the composition of the candidate pool at key decision points in the selection process. Perhaps you will notice a pattern that will inform future searches.

One search committee surveyed the candidates who made it to the second and third round interviews and asked about their impressions of the process and suggestions for improvement. We strongly advocate that you take the time to evaluate your process and share what you learn from your analysis with HR, the decision maker, and the campus as a whole. It is likely that your experience will improve another department's search or enrich the diversity of the institution's applicant pools. We believe it is important for institutions to keep a record of good practices and successful searches for future reference.

As part of their initiative to recruit more women and minorities to faculty positions in engineering, the University of Michigan suggests these questions to evaluate the process:

- If the department hires a woman and/or minority candidate, ask: What were the factors that may have enabled it to do so?
- If the applicant pool was not as large, as qualified, or as diverse as was anticipated, ask:
  - Could the job description have been constructed in a way that would have brought in a broader pool of candidates?
  - Could the department have recruited more actively?
  - Were there criteria for this position that were consistently not met by women or candidates of color?
- If women and/or minority candidates were offered positions that they chose not to accept, ask: What reasons did they offer? Consider as many factors as you can identify.

Checklist for Negotiating and Making the Offer

- ❒ Compiled known and easily obtained salary and compensation data from comparable institutions
- ❒ Shared information with the decision maker, HR
- ❒ Specifically sold the candidates and significant others on the opportunity
- ❒ Prepared best case scenarios on each candidate, including areas of concern and recommendations, and presented finalists to the decision maker
- ❒ Sought out and addressed concerns from the candidates and their partners
- ❒ Sent letters to the other finalists after the offer has been accepted
- ❒ Completed forms required for HR, AA, or Diversity offices
- ❒ Evaluated the process and shared the findings with the decision maker, HR, and appropriate campus contacts

- Are there things that the department could do to make it more attractive to desirable candidates in the future? Be sure that any analysis and insight are shared with departmental decision makers and recommend that future searches incorporate your findings.

Celebrate!

At the point where the candidates are presented to the decision maker, your official work is done. The search committee is often informed of the outcome before the formal announcement. The decision maker may request that you join in announcing the candidate to the institution and the community, where relevant. In many institutions, the decision maker thanks the search committee by taking them to dinner to celebrate a job well done, or extending another similar gesture of appreciation. The chair may send notes of appreciation to each of the members and recognize their contributions in notes for their personnel or tenure files.

We encourage you to take the time to celebrate your contribution to the campus and the opportunity to collaborate with colleagues in ways that extend your relationship beyond ordinary contact. Perhaps you will enjoy an expanded professional relationship and even a twenty-year friendship, as we have, from your collegial interactions on this search.

Furthermore, the potential for the search committee to contribute to the long-term vitality of the campus could be realized if you were open to expanding your role after the offer has been accepted. We encourage you to continue your involvement with the selected candidate by creating and implementing "intentional and random acts of hospitality," and to contribute what you learned to the college retention plan. Ideas for expanding your role are developed in the final chapter.

Potential Pitfalls

- **Leaving the candidate and significant others adrift**. Emotional and informational support is crucial at this stage. The candidate needs to know there is someone in his or her corner, and engaging the partner is a key factor in choosing to accept an offer.
- **Not doing your homework.** Make sure that HR and the decision maker have all the information you have gleaned and can cull that would help them make the best offer to the candidate.
- **Not making a compelling case to the decision maker**. Your knowledge of the candidate

and the position are more complete than that of anyone else at the institution. Give the decision maker your best recommendations and the most complete information available about the finalists.

- **Failing to learn from your lessons and sharing lessons learned with the campus.** Your evaluation of the process adds invaluable knowledge to the search committee process of the institution. Wherever possible, share your wisdom with others. The payoffs in terms of streamlined processes, effective decisions, new hire retention, and student satisfaction are incalculable.
- **Neglecting to inform the other finalists of the decision in a timely manner.** The impact you make on those not chosen for the position will affect your reputation and the reputation of your institution in future searches.

References

Faculty Recruitment Handbook, NSF Advance at the University of Michigan Academic Year 2004–2005. Retrieved 02/24/05 from www.umich.edu/~advproj/handbook.pdf

Sample Summaries of Finalists, Virginia Polytechnic Institute and State University, retrieved 02/24/05 from www.eoaa.vt.edu/Search/finalizing.pdf

CHAPTER 10

Extending Hospitality to the New Hire

In this chapter, you will

- Entertain an expanded role for the search committee
- Consider examples of ways that other search committees have extended hospitality
- Identify ways to contribute to the retention of new hires

Getting Started

GREAT NEWS! The new hire has accepted the offer and, if your institution is like most others, your work on the search committee is complete. Or is it?

If there were simple and personally gratifying ways that you and the other committee members could contribute to retaining the new hire and to growing the institution, would you choose to do them? If your answer is yes, even a tentative yes, this chapter is for you.

These simple, personally gratifying ways to ensure the return on your investment are "intentional acts of hospitality." Yet, the practice of extending hospitality to the new hire is neither expected nor prevalent. So why do it?

Investing in Hospitality

In our experience, there are two sound reasons for the search committee to assume this responsibility. First, taking deliberate steps to make the new hire feel welcomed and wanted on your campus and in your local community is like taking out an insurance policy. Your investment in hospitality will pay off. The new member is much more likely to fit in, to assimilate more easily, to contribute more vitally and quickly to the campus and the community, and to feel a kinship with other members of both communities. In addition, the stress experienced by the new hire's family members will also be greatly diminished. Both of these factors translate economically as well as emotionally/psychologically into a wise investment.

The second reason is that new hires, especially those who come from underrepresented groups, are more likely to stay and to attract others to the institution—faculty, administrators, and students—if they themselves feel welcomed. This, too, pays off economically as well as psychologically. Intentional acts of hospitality improve the morale and enhance the reputation of your campus in the greater academic community.

As Dr. Fred Bonner, Associate Professor of Adult and Higher Education at the University of Texas San Antonio noted in a recent *Chronicle* article on minority faculty, "No faculty member can be successful without establishing professional networks—that is, being included in the higher-education loop. Unfortunately, for many African American faculty members, gaining access to the loop is difficult, if not impossible." While he was referring to one specific group, underrepresented groups include women, members of cultural and ethnic minority groups, homosexuals, and people with disabilities. Anecdotal evidence suggests that academic environments are likely to be not only indifferent but actually inhospitable to them. Some colleagues assume that offices like Student Services or Diversity/Minority Affairs address their needs, but these resources serve students rather than faculty and staff.

Whether the new hire is from an underrepresented

group or not, simple acts of hospitality, spearheaded by the search committee, are highly likely to affect the relationship between the new hire and the department and to change the campus climate in very positive ways.

Appreciating the Historical Roots of Hospitality

The roots of our current practices of hospitality originate from ancient nomadic tribes in the Middle East. In such forbidding desert areas, the offer of hospitality was a life or death decision. It was customary for nomadic people to open their tents and share all their belongings, indeed the best of what they possessed, with strangers who came to them. Over time the practice of hospitality became a sacred duty, not a social grace. It was thought that the stranger who was welcomed brought precious gifts. The Biblical story of Abraham and Sarah exemplifies this belief. "Do not neglect to show hospitality to the stranger, for thereby some have entertained angels."

These Judeo-Christian and Islamic roots of hospitality form the foundation of our beliefs and practices in relation to those who are strangers to us. Genuine hospitality is not exclusive, it is inclusive. It means creating a free space where the stranger can enter and become an intimate friend instead of an enemy. The dynamic of hospitality is not to change people but to offer them space where change can take place. By creating space for a large variety of human experience, we can receive the experiences of others as a gift to us. Their histories connect with ours, and their lives give meaning to ours.

Most of us have come to think of hospitality on the level of a housewarming gift, flowers for the new job, or a visit by the Welcome Wagon. Each of these practices, and others like them, are fine rituals that nurture good feelings and lubricate relationships. Practicing hospitality at that level with a new hire will make a difference, especially if more than one person participates. However, if the gestures remain at the superficial level, the new hire may feel like an "other," relegated to the guest room and separated from the family.

What if you chose to take hospitality to a deeper level? You might contribute to creating a campus culture that truly welcomes strangers as their honored guests and celebrates the gifts that their presence brings. Such practices of hospitality address the deeper issues of personal and psychological safety, belonging, nurturing, and healing. When practiced in this deeper way, guests become family.

What could you do to precipitate intentional acts of hospitality on your campus? Here are some ideas to consider.

Defining Hospitality on Your Campus

Many definitions of hospitality exist. A few are listed on page 89. Consider dialoguing about the meaning of hospitality with the members of the search committee or the department which the new hire will join. Which definitions resonate with your campus culture and your intentions in welcoming the new hire? How could you and the hiring department transform the meaning of hospitality into a practice?

Exploring the Practices of Hospitality

Over time, the practice of extending hospitality may become an accepted part of the search committees and the hiring departments on your campus. Imagine if you were the new hire. What gestures of friendship and welcome would you appreciate from your new colleagues? What could they do or say that would help you feel comfortable, included, and wanted?

Gestures of hospitality don't need to be extravagant, cost a lot of money or time, or entangle you in relationships that you don't want to cultivate. Following are two true stories that illustrate aspects of hospitality. These are followed by some ideas gleaned from colleagues at several different institutions. Which ones do you think the search committee might be willing to put into action? Which might the search committee be willing to suggest to others on campus?

Leslie's Story: Afternoon Tea

I was the only woman in the chemistry department at my new college. During the first month of my contract, an English Department professor invited me to Sunday tea at her house. It turned out that a group of senior women faculty at the college met once a month for Sunday tea. They began the practice to stay in touch with other women who had retired from the College. In late September, they expanded their tea group for one meeting to include all the new women faculty who had been hired that year. I met new and experienced professors from psychology, English, religious studies, biology, and communications. None of the new faculty had met before, even during orientation, so it was a chance to meet some of the senior faculty as well as a number of my peers. The agenda included a general introduction of each member of the group as well as a discussion of major issues that faced the faculty at the college. I had a chance to meet the faculty member I had replaced, and she gave me some tips on dealing with the chemistry lab preps. The Sunday Tea for New Faculty has become an annual event. All my new colleagues agreed that the tea was a very significant factor in solidifying our acclimation to the college and the community.

Arturo's Story

We had just moved to a small-town college, several hundred miles away from the nearest family and friends. I was glad I had my partner with me. It would've been hard to move to a new place totally alone.

Within hours of moving into our new apartment, we had a knock on the door. Another new faculty member from my department had moved in with his wife to the same apartment complex, and our department chair had told him which apartment we were in. It was a great surprise and wonderful to meet another couple new to the area. The next day, we were invited to a department picnic at the lake cottage of one of the faculty. We went boating, swam in the lake, and toasted marshmallows over the campfire. It was a chance for us to get acquainted in a casual setting. It was a great introduction to our new home and my new colleagues.

Behind the familiar rituals of hospitality exists a certain structure as outlined in the box on page 90. This structure applies to a single event of hospitality as well as the ongoing practice of hospitality. Let's look at each practice and examine examples of intentional acts of hospitality from each one that have been extended at various other institutions. Which ones might be possible for you or your committee to do?

Welcoming the New Hire

- Meet the new hire when she arrives in town. Take some food, present a gift certificate to a community restaurant, or invite her and her family to join you for a meal at your home.
- Bring flowers, a welcome banner, a basket of goodies, or some other small gift for her office.

What is Hospitality?

- Hospitality is making someone feel at home.
- The core of hospitality is universalizing the neighbor and personalizing the stranger.
- Hospitality is the attitude and practice of providing the atmosphere and opportunity, however risky, in which strangers are free to become friends, thereby feeling accepted, included, and deeply valued.
- Hospitality is not fine accoutrements, the "Sunday best." It is the invitation, the welcome, the act of extending shelter that includes—this is what matters most to people.
- The whole concept of hospitality is built around the idea of serving one another. With hospitality we create the space where guests feel at home with us and themselves. This means not only being receptive to guests but, when appropriate, confronting unacceptable behavior and setting and sticking to limits.
- Hospitality is the movement in which we become less fearful and defensive and more open to the other.
- Hospitality is a reciprocal relationship intent on friendship and respect. It is a lively, courageous, and convivial way of living that is inclusive and not isolationary.
- Hospitality is more than a happening. It is a value, an attitude, an expectation, a way of approaching life. We expect guests. We are ready to receive them. We are prepared to offer them our best. We expect to be blessed. That very attitude changes our behavior.

The Practices of Hospitality

- Welcome the guest/stranger
- Extend resources
- Respond to their physical, social, emotional, and spiritual needs
- Share food and drink at a common table
- Assure their safety
- Listen to their stories and share yours

- Arrange for members of the department to take him to coffee or lunch on his first day.
- Organize an informal welcoming gathering of students and department members on her first day at work.
- Send a "welcome to the department /university" card to his home, personally signed.
- Arrange for students and department members to give her a personal tour and make appropriate introductions to people and resources.
- Write a short press release for the campus and community newspapers to introduce him. Consider posting his introduction on the websites of the institution and department.
- Arrange for her to be interviewed for a short feature story for the campus or community newspaper.

Extend Resources

- Stock his office with fresh supplies.
- Arrange for the office administrator to meet with her soon after her arrival to order materials and supplies.
- Suggest that the department head/manager review the guidelines on travel, reimbursements, subscriptions, and other resources that he might use in the near future.
- Offer to expedite the paperwork related to her move.
- Organize a gathering that includes the spouse or partner to share the best restaurants, shopping places, churches, auto mechanics, day care centers, physicians and health care, bookstores, cleaners, theaters, etc.
- Provide him with a month's parking pass and a gift certificate for the campus bookstore.

Respond to Needs / Ensure Safety

- Check in after a few weeks and inquire how he is doing and what would make his life easier.
- Search out campus or community resources that are likely to satisfy a need of the new hire or a member of the family. One search committee identified ice hockey options for a new director with two teenage sons who were avid hockey players.
- Introduce her to community leaders and organizations that share her interests. A member of one search committee accompanied a new minority administrator to a racially integrated neighborhood meeting and introduced her to key Black leaders in the community. Soon after, she moved into that neighborhood and became active in that very organization.
- Arrange an introduction to Campus Security, to point out any areas of concern, the way to secure an escort, the location of the emergency phones. Especially on large urban campuses, it helps her acclimation and sense of safety.
- Facilitate his psychological safety by filling him in on "the rules of the game."

Share a Meal / Listen to Stories

- After a month or so, invite him for coffee or lunch; ask how he's doing and if he needs anything.

- Introduce and encourage other members of the campus community to invite her for coffee or lunch.
- Provide a voucher for him to invite students to lunch.
- Inquire from Human Resources about other recent new hires. Suggest that HR sponsor a new hires gathering so they can meet each other.
- Organize a tea, an outing, or other special event to introduce colleagues and stimulate conversation.

Hospitality has the power to transform people, organizations, and communities—as well as those who extend it (you!). Accepting and including newcomers creates the space for them to share who they are with you, and you to share yourself with them. And hospitality reaches beyond the new hires. You have the power to effect positive change—indeed to transform the campus climate by starting in small, intentional ways. Imagine what would happen if even incoming students were welcomed as if they were "angels to be entertained!"

Contributing to Retention Planning

You learned a great deal from participating on the search committee—valuable insights about your institution, its strengths and areas of concern, others' perceptions, and comparisons with similar institutions. You also know the new hire better than anyone on campus, and your insights about the factors that would make the person feel welcomed, wanted, and valued may be critical to his or her retention. By advocating with the hiring authority or appropriate institutional department for including the salient factors in the new hire's professional development plan, you not only contribute to the person's retention, you support the practice of retention planning on your campus. Doesn't it seem like a waste not to pass this on and put it to good use? Who needs to know and use this information?

While it is beyond the scope of the search committee to take on retention planning, you could serve as a bridge to those responsible for it. Does your college have a retention plan? Many colleges and universities have established retention plans for new hires, and several, such as Auburn University's College of Engineering, have plans specifically targeting minority and female hires. Has your school established specific measures to monitor its progress in recruitment, retention, and promotion of new hires?

Planning for retention strengthens the institution and benefits all members of the community. The list of suggested activities on page 92, typical components of a retention program, may be important to your new hire.

An End Note

Serving on search committees that select the best qualified people for positions is an especially satisfying role. However, one sure way to demoralize staff is to ask them to serve on a search committee but not support their work. If an institution cannot retain the people they so carefully sought and selected, few staff will be motivated to serve on a search committee. Extending hospitality to the new hire provides an insurance policy for your investment. It may inspire your administration to pursue a retention plan where no formal one is yet in place. Your attention to the small details of welcoming new members of the community may profoundly change the campus climate for colleagues and students alike in unexpectedly propitious ways. One of the greatest satisfactions is seeing the fruits of your intense committee work—the contributions that your new hires make to the legacy of the institution because they love what they do and where they work.

And since all good work should be acknowledged and rewarded, we encourage you to celebrate your accomplishment and recognize the valuable contribution your work has made to the vitality of the campus community.

References

Bonner F. (2004). Black professors: On the track but out of the loop. *The Chronicle of Higher Education, 50*(40), B11.

Minority Faculty Recruiting and Retention Plan, Auburn University Samuel Ginn College of Engineering Retrieved on 02/24/05 from www.eng.auburn.edu/admin/planning/mfrrp/

Successful Retention Activities

- Mentoring programs for new faculty, teaming them with senior faculty, perhaps those of the same gender or from similar racial or ethnic backgrounds
- Formal contact between junior and senior faculty, such as planned collaboration in teaching
- Professional development programs for new faculty that enhance their preparation for the tenure process
- Ongoing professional development programs for all faculty and staff, including sponsorship of campus-wide multicultural and diversity activities for staff, faculty, and students
- Regular communication with the professional staff and faculty about issues related to recruitment, strategies used at other institutions, and climate issues
- Identification of funding sources for fellowship programs and other programs designed to focus on issues related to diversity
- Financial support, funding, and release time for research projects
- Workloads and compensation that recognize that members of underrepresented groups often have heavier demands than do their colleagues for serving on committees and representing their cultural experiences and perspectives as participants in campus and community events
- Opportunities for informal contact between and among faculty members from various disciplines and cultural groups to foster cross-fertilization, collaboration, and a more positive campus climate
- Opportunities to engage the institution in cluster hiring or spousal hiring practices that might attract a more diverse candidate pool
- Exit interviews to determine why faculty and staff choose to leave and to monitor the impact on the diversity of the staff/faculty
- Rewards for faculty and staff who are involved in research related to diversity issues such as multiculturalism, gender, ethnicity, and race
- Rewards for faculty who are actively engaged in tutoring, mentoring, outreach activities, counseling, recruitment and retention of students
- Rewards for faculty who are engaged in developing and piloting pedagogical techniques designed to accommodate diverse learning styles
- Rewards for faculty and staff who have made their classroom/office welcoming to students and members of the campus community
- Flexible approaches to accommodating faculty/staff special needs such as childcare/eldercare time, medical leave, parental leave, etc.
- Publicly supporting the value of diversity and the importance of welcoming all new members to the campus community (including students)
- Joint appointments with ethnic and women's studies programs to advance research, pedagogy and curriculum development that address issues of gender, diversity, and new areas of learning.

For Further Reading

Bernal, Martha E. (1996). *Valuing diversity: A faculty guide.* Washington DC: The American Psychological Association.

Caldwell-Colbert, A. Toy (1996). *How to recruit and hire ethnic minority faculty.* Washington DC: The American Psychological Association.

Castellanos, J., & Jones, L. (Eds.) (2003). *The Majority in the minority: Expanding the representation of Latina/o faculty, administrators, and students in higher education.* Sterling VA.: Stylus

Committee on Women in Psychology and APA Commission on Ethnic Minority Recruitment, Retention, and Training in Psychology (1998). *Surviving and thriving in academia: A guide for women and ethnic minorities.* Washington DC: American Psychological Association.

Davis, L. (2002). Racial Diversity in Higher Education. *Journal of Applied Behavioral Science, 38*(2), 137–155.

Jones, L. (Ed.) (2001). *Retaining African Americans in higher education: Challenging paradigms for retaining students, faculty and administrators.* Sterling VA: Stylus.

Marchese, T. J., with Lawrence, F. J. (1998). *The search committee handbook: A guide to recruiting administrators.* Washington DC: American Association for Higher Education.

Perlman, B., & McCann L. I.(1996). *Recruiting good college faculty.* Bolton MA: Anker.

Roach, R. (2001). Is higher education ready for minority America? *Black Issues in Higher Education, 18*(8), 29–31.

Rosse, J. G., & Levin, R. A. (2002*) The Jossey-Bass academic administrator's guide to hiring.* San Francisco: Jossey-Bass/Pfeiffer

Stewart, C. J., & Cash, W. B. (2002). *Interviewing: Principles and practices* (10th ed.). Boston: McGraw-Hill.

Still, D. (2001). *High impact hiring: How to interview and select outstanding employees* (2nd ed.) Dana Point CA: Management Development Systems.

Turner, C. S. (2002). *Diversifying the faculty: A guidebook for search committees.* Washington DC: Association of American Colleges and Universities.

Turner, C. (1994). Guests in someone else's house: Students of color on campus. *The Review of Higher Education, 17*(4), 355–370.

Wilson, R. F. (1997). *Conducting better job interviews* (2nd ed.). Hauppauge NY: Barron's Educational Series, Inc.

Additional Web Sites Worth Noting

American Association for Higher Education diversity resources
www.aahe.org/diversityresources.htm

American Association of Colleges and Universities, diversity resources
http://aacu.org/issues/diversity/index.cfm

American Association of University Women
http://aauw.org

Diversity 2004 Conference Proceedings, Greater Rochester Diversity Council
www.rochesterdiversitycouncil.com

Diversity Digest, an online periodical
www.diversityweb.org/digest/

Historically Black Colleges and Universities
www.hbcunetwork.com/

Michigan State University, Academic Hiring Manual
www.hr.msu.edu/HRsite/Documents/Faculty/Handbooks/Hiring/

University of California, Santa Barbara, Law Prohibiting Discrimination
http://hr.ucsb.edu/Labor/discrimination.htm

University of Illinois, College of Liberal Arts and Sciences, Academic Professional and Faculty Hiring Procedures
www.d.umn.edu/umdoeo/guide.html

University of Minnesota Duluth, Guidelines for Academic Hiring
www.d.umn.edu/umdoeo/guide.html

Index

Contacting Us

If you have further questions you would like addressed, or if you have a story to share or an Example Worth Noting to offer, please contact us at academicsearch@yahoo.com. We will do our best to respond promptly to your concerns, and we welcome your comments on the search process we have described here.